IN PRAISE OF 'A GUIDE FOR LIFE'

"*A Guide for Life* provides an important service to people who are seeking personal guidance in the bewildering world of self-help!"

~ Rob Williams
Originator of PSYCH-K®, Author

"You have put so much energy into *A Guide for Life*! I love the name and I wish I'd had a resource like this 30 years ago!!"

~ Gregg Braden
Best-selling author, Nominee 2019 Templeton Award

"Wow! What an immense amount of work and love you have put into *A Guide for Life*. You've done such a stellar job. Congratulations!! I can only begin to imagine how much effort it all has taken."

~ Denise Linn
Soul Coach, International Lecturer & Healer

"I am really impressed. You have done the work. You have been able to bring all of that into your own story. That's why it's so powerful. Because it's not just you telling your story; it's you shining the light on people who helped you get there. You've really nailed it. This (*A Guide for Life*) is going to resonate with so many people who are 'looking'. That's what people need. You have connected all the dots. You've hit the key points. You've got the right tools. You've got the leaders in the field. You are giving people not only the information (they need) but allowing them to pick and choose what they think they need. It's really tremendous."

~ Dr Jeffrey Fannin
Neuroscientist, Author, Speaker, Researcher

BUILD A LIFE YOU LOVE: WORKBOOK #1

FIND YOUR PURPOSE, CHANGE YOUR LIFE

A guide for uncovering your life's calling to create a joyous, fulfilling and meaningful life

Kylie Attwell

Title: FIND YOUR PURPOSE, CHANGE YOUR LIFE: A guide for uncovering your life's calling to create a joyous, fulfilling and meaningful life.

©Kylie Attwell 2019

The moral rights of Kylie Attwell to be identified as the author of this work have been asserted in accordance with the Copyright Act 1968.

First published in Australia 2019 by A Guide for Life
www.aguideforlife.com

ISBN 978-0-64857-731-7

Any opinions expressed in this work are exclusively those of the author.

Disclaimer
The content of this workbook is published for educational and informational purposes only. The content of this workbook is not intended to provide personalised financial, career, medical, psychological, spiritual or therapeutic advice. The content of this book should not be used for the diagnosis or treatment of any condition or disease. Readers are advised to seek the counsel of competent professionals with regards such matters, especially chronic depression, mental, psychological and emotional instability, financial planning and career planning. The Author and Publisher specifically disclaim any liability, loss, or risk which is incurred as a consequence, directly or indirectly, of the use and application of any of the contents of this work.

To the souls who feel as lost, empty and depressed as I did prior to setting out on my journey of self-discovery, and to the teachers who helped transform my life.

ABOUT KYLIE ATTWELL

Kylie Attwell is a content curator and facilitator for self-transformation. Her skills and services take a multi-disciplinary approach and incorporate the latest therapeutic modalities and brain science. In her Brisbane practice, she provides clients with personalised guidance and offers hands-on healing sessions to relieve stress and anxiety. She also facilitates belief change and emotional release sessions to help change the printout of their lives.

Despite where she is today, Kylie didn't always know herself or her purpose. While seemingly living the ideal life and having built a successful career in Medical Imaging, she battled depression, anxiety and emptiness. After ending up almost broke (both emotionally and financially) by mistaking a passion for her purpose, she started working on herself. Thousands of hours and dollars later, Kylie discovered one simple truth: "The reason my life felt unfulfilling and empty was because it lacked real purpose and meaning."

The next stage of her journey involved using the techniques in this workbook to discover her life purpose. The framework Kylie presents evolved as a result of her discovering that no one self-development or spiritual teacher has all the answers. Her aim in developing this workbook is therefore to help others avoid the long and costly path she took.

In addition, Kylie has developed the website, aguideforlife.com, as the hub for her work and a free online resource for others. Gregg Braden, best-selling author and pioneer in bridging science, spirituality and human potential, has lauded this website as one of the best of its kind in the world. He professed, "I wish I'd had a resource like this 30 years ago!"

When Kylie is not helping clients, she continues to focus on completing the *Build a Life You Love Workbook Series* – seven workbooks presenting all the information, tools and techniques that gave her the freedom to express herself fully across all aspects of her life.

Contact:
Kylie Attwell
+61 410 564 000
kylie@aguideforlife.com

WHY THIS WORKBOOK?

Not so long ago I felt adrift and disenchanted by life, despite my perceived success. What I craved was a meaningful, deeply fulfilling and joyous life, but it eluded me, regardless of how hard I tried. With so much information out there in the human potential and personal development sectors, as well as the psychology and self-help sections in bookstores, I found it difficult to determine what resources would lead to real and lasting change when seeking to improve my life circumstances.

Fortunately that paradigm is far behind me now. Don't get me wrong; my life still has its challenges and there are issues I continue to wrestle with, but my life now has direction and meaning. I also possess the tools and the self-confidence to deal with anything that crosses my path. Each day my life is becoming richer, more colourful and joyous. That is my wish for you!

Searching for an answer

You might be like I once was, trying one thing after another but not really knowing what you are looking for. By the time I'd reached my late twenties I'd incorporated everything that I thought would make me happy into my life: a secure and lucrative career, dream house, classic car, busy social life, designer things and heaps of 'friends'. I was supposed to feel happy and fulfilled, right? Except I wasn't. I felt hollow and deeply unhappy. Was there something wrong with me?

I concluded that there was no real joy in my life, so I followed my heart and set up a business based on my love for architecture and design. Soon afterwards Prince Charming arrived on the scene. Yet, deep down I still felt empty inside.

Fast forward ten years, the fairy-tale romance had ended and I'd closed my business. I was freshly divorced and now broke, both emotionally and financially. I felt like a complete failure. What now?

Being a logical person I went searching for what was 'missing'. I changed career three more times. I spent thousands of dollars on books, seminars, workshops and retreats. Yet I still felt lost and confused about what would truly make me happy. I hit rock bottom.

A turning point

After searching high and low for sixteen years, I finally came across key people (or I could say the Universe sent them) who helped me identify what was missing in my life; that is, a sense of purpose. These people and their work helped me to uncover my reason for living and encouraged me to live in alignment with that purpose. That's when my life started to change dramatically, and quickly, in my early forties.

Once I'd found and owned my purpose, I started removing the distractions, emotional baggage and self-limiting beliefs that were creating friction in my life. By doing so, I could think more clearly and my inner voice began to emerge. As I started to express my needs and desires my life unfolded with more ease. My confidence and sense of fulfilment grew with every new step I took towards embodying my life purpose – my reason for living, my zone of genius, my life calling, the theme of my hero's journey.

I finally realised I didn't need to become someone else to step into my life's purpose: it's who I already was at my very core. This is also a central message of many great spiritual teachers. All I needed to know was where to look and what questions to ask myself. The more I developed an intimate relationship with myself, the more I began to trust expressing myself fully in the world at large. The journey of self-discovery will strip away who you are not, so you are finally free to be your authentic self across every aspect of your life.

What you will gain

This workbook is one of seven that I have created to help you successfully build a life you love. That life is one which truly embodies your long-held desires and dreams. It is deeply fulfilling and provides you a with sense of purpose and, importantly, the freedom to fully express yourself in every area of your life: career; relationships; home environment; physical appearance; lifestyle; hobbies; social activities; and interests.

In other words, you get to create a *joyous, meaningful and fulfilling life*, in which *you are free to be all of you*.

Sound too good to be true? As a lifelong sufferer of anxiety and depression, I never thought it was possible to feel content, fully present and awed by life on a daily basis. My mother tells me that even as a tiny baby I used to projectile vomit the moment I perceived any tension in the room, and for as long as I can remember I was plagued with a deep sense of melancholy that rarely left me. I also lived in constant fear of getting into trouble for doing something wrong or unintentionally hurting someone.

As a consequence, I did exactly as I was told and became a people pleaser. However, that all started to change at 42, when I began actively working my way through the material and activities I have collated within this series of workbooks.

This first workbook is designed to help you accurately identify the themes of your life calling and assist you to recognise the ways in which you are already naturally expressing them. It will also help you determine what you value most in life and who you aspire to be.

Discovering your life purpose is the crucial first step to build a life you love. This workbook offers you a clear-cut, direct path to knowing yourself and your purpose, saving you from the long and expensive trial-and-error route I took. Overall, the goal of this workbook is to help you live an inspired, purposeful and deeply satisfying life.

Rather than delving deeply into the benefits of uncovering your life purpose, which is the focus of other books on this topic, my aim is to direct you to key information and get you working straight away, before you lose momentum. The activities I prescribe (only five!) are designed to reveal your life purpose quickly.

If you are curious by nature and would like to read more about the rationale and rewards of discovering your life calling, the *Inspirational Resources* section at the back of this workbook references resources that provide you with in-depth knowledge of this topic. They include examples of everyday people and historic icons who found and embodied their life purpose. These resources also contain an extensive number of supplementary exercises and self-enquiry questions to help you gain an even deeper understanding of yourself. You can never know yourself too well!

The self-discovery process set out in this workbook is the methodology I followed. For me, it proved to be invaluable and limitless in its potential. I was often surprised by what I discovered the more I got to know myself! For instance, I rediscovered parts of myself I'd forgotten and uncovered interests and hobbies that I didn't even know I liked, let alone loved, plus new and preferred ways of doing things. My sincere hope is that you too will gain as much, if not more, from these processes.

Who is this workbook for?

Are you one of those lucky people who have always known what you wanted to be when you grew up, but are still not able to gain traction in your desired field and are supplementing your income through unrelated work? If the answer to this question is yes, it would be worth taking the time to work through the following material to accurately confirm the theme of your life calling.

If this workbook validates that your field of choice is congruent with the theme of your life's purpose, you can be confident in knowing you are on the right path. Your lack of traction can then be addressed by removing any self-limiting beliefs and trapped emotions that are keeping you stuck and blocking your path to success. *The instructions for doing so are covered in detail within the subsequent workbooks.*

On the other hand, if it's revealed that the theme of your purpose differs from the field you have been passionately pursuing, it means your course needs to be redirected so that it aligns with your true calling. This change of focus does not mean that you need to give up your passions – they play an essential role in our lives. However, it's important that you don't mistake a passion for your life purpose, which I will explain in detail in the *Introduction* section. Rather, it's about consciously incorporating your passions into your day-to-day life to generate uplifting feelings that help to support you as you begin to chart your new course. *More will be covered on this process in subsequent workbooks, and I strongly recommend you work through the entire series.*

This workbook is definitely for you if you:

- are preparing to leave school, or have recently left, and are seeking career or study direction
- are dissatisfied with your job and your life
- want to go back into the workforce after an extended break

- wish to make a meaningful change in your occupation
- have lost direction and are unsure what to do with your life
- have lost your enthusiasm for life and feel stuck
- lack energy and struggle to get out of bed in the morning
- are simply working to make ends meet and have no passion for your work
- feel bored more often than not
- are on autopilot and 'sleepwalk' through your workday
- find your work unfulfilling and spend your day watching the clock
- feel exhausted at the end of each day
- live for the weekend then dread Monday morning
- feel you have nothing to live for
- suffer chronic depression.

I can certainly attribute my battle with depression to having no mission in life or reason for living. My bouts of melancholy and chronic depression, which I recall experiencing from as young as two, lifted permanently once I began to live in alignment with who I truly am and embodied my life purpose.

Psychologists now believe that addiction, to some extent, arises due to a lack of purpose or meaning. When we have a keen sense of purpose, we are more resilient to life's challenges and can overcome setbacks or childhood trauma. Conversely, when we have no reason for living, we are more susceptible to depression and are more likely to reach for alcohol and drugs or take up other addictive behaviours to escape feelings of boredom, frustration, pessimism and loneliness that surface when life doesn't meet our expectations.

Research now demonstrates that recovery from addiction is more likely to last if the individual establishes a sense of purpose in their life. For this reason, I highly recommend this workbook if you have any behavioural or substance addictions related but not limited to:

- alcohol
- co-dependency
- food and energy drinks
- gambling
- illegal and/or prescription drugs
- love
- sex
- shopping
- smoking
- social media and internet
- sugar.

Guiding the way

I am not a certified therapist or career counsellor, nor do I consider myself a coach. I see my role more as a content curator for self-transformation and a guide or mentor. My intention is to point you in the direction of the resources, people and tools that I believe can be truly effective in helping you, just as they helped me.

This workbook gives you everything you need to discover your life purpose. The methodologies presented are not based on theory and hope. They are proven methods and practical tools used by career advisors, psychologists, specialists in human behaviour and human potential, and elite personal development coaches and mentors.

Based on my research and personal self-transformation journey, I believe this workbook is by far the most definitive and comprehensive work on this subject. It contains the information, activities and exercises I used to successfully determine the themes of my life's calling. Family, friends, former work colleagues and clients have also gained clarity around their reason for living through completing the material.

Doing this work will take time and effort, but I assure you the rewards far outweigh the effort required. Since finding and living my calling, I've consistently felt emotionally buoyant and joyous. For the first time in my life, I now experience true inner contentment and a deep sense of peace.

Uncovering your life purpose and living in alignment with it is the most precious gift you can give yourself. It provides a reason for everything you do in life. Aside from improving the quality, research suggests that having purpose can even extend the length of your life. It's the difference between you simply existing and living a meaningful, joyous and fulfilling life.

CONTENTS

INTRODUCTION

Welcome! This workbook, the first in the *Build a Life You Love* series, is designed to provide you with both an objective and subjective approach to identifying the themes of your life purpose – the first crucial step in creating a meaningful, joyous and deeply satisfying life.

Think of this workbook as a form of 'curriculum' or 'syllabus' to achieve these goals. It summarises why discovering your purpose is critical to living an inspiring and fulfilling life, and then outlines the activities you need to complete to accurately identify and embrace your life's calling – including the 'textbooks' required and an 'excursion' you'll need to take. It provides you with the space to record your answers, reflections and feelings about what you have uncovered, and helps you to collate and process this information to gain a clear picture of your overall WHY in life.

I can assure you that you have everything inside of yourself right now to discover your reason for being. I will be walking right beside you throughout the entire process.

USING THIS WORKBOOK

There is no right or wrong way to complete this workbook. My advice is to complete what resonates with you and leave the rest. What's most important is that you complete as much as you need to gain a clear picture of the themes of your life's calling. If you already know yourself well, you may find that you only need to complete one of the five activities. However, if you are new to the self-development sector you might need to work through the entire workbook.

The process of self-discovery is not meant to be a chore. It's meant to be a fun and exciting adventure. After all, it's all about you and getting to know you. This is a sacred process that's meant to be enjoyed and savoured.

Create space for yourself

You will need to set aside time to do this self-exploration work, free of distraction. I suggest you turn off your mobile phone and seclude yourself in a quiet and nurturing environment where you won't be disturbed.

In today's hectic world, finding time to do the work all at once may not be possible, nor is it necessary. Instead, you may benefit from setting aside specific and regular times. For example:

- 30 minutes before work, during your lunch break or immediately after dinner to complete an activity question
- a few hours on Sunday afternoons to finish an entire activity
- a whole day or weekend to complete all of the workbook activities.

Whatever you do, carve out the time and create space to discover the purpose of your existence. Trust me, it's worth it!

The devil is in the distractions

Expect all kinds of distractions to arise when doing this self-exploration work. The reason? It can be frightening to spend quality time with yourself. Change from the status quo can be perceived as threatening to your mind, which is hardwired to ensure your safety. As a result, all forms of diversions and disturbances can occur as a way of 'protecting' you from doing the inner-work. Be alert of interlopers, the tendency to procrastinate, unforseen emergencies or the sudden onset of an illness. All of these are signs of your subconscious resistance to change.

I encourage you to persist, regardless of the obstructions and interference you encounter. If self-direction is not one of your strong points, it may be helpful to invite a friend to do the processes with you, thereby establishing an accountability partner. In my experience, you can benefit greatly by joining forces with others who share the dream of living a meaningful life. It can be a powerful and effective way to facilitate progress and obtain results.

FIVE ACTIVITIES TO UNCOVER YOUR PURPOSE

Activity 1 is *The Demartini Values Determination Process* by Dr. John Demartini, a world-renowned specialist in human behaviour. The process involves answering 13 questions about your core behaviours and passions to help you identify what you are most passionate about and hold in high regard. Discovering this information not only gives you clues to your life purpose; it also allows you to identify what you value most. Understanding this gives you the foundations when it comes time to designing and constructing the life you've always dreamed of living. *The design and build phase is the focus of Workbooks 2–7.*

Activity 2 requires you to answer five questions about your deepest desires, the types of activities that inspire you and the people you admire, to help reveal more about who you are at your core and the person you aspire to be.

Activity 3 involves having an astrological analysis to accurately define the themes of your life purpose. This is done in a consultation with Narelle Duncan, a highly acclaimed and award-winning professional astrologer specialising in career direction and relationship counselling, with whom I consulted. Narelle holds a Bachelor of Psychology with 1st Class Honours, a Diploma of Astrology (a nationally recognised qualification issued by the Federation of Australian Astrologers) and is now completing her Doctorate in Clinical Psychology. She has been using her counselling skills and natural perceptive abilities to help people discover their life purpose and live their 'best life' for more than 25 years.

You'll walk away from this one-hour consultation knowing the themes of your life purpose, along with personalised, practical and relatable examples of how you can live in alignment with your life's calling. In this section I will also shed some light on astrology, which Carl Gustav Jung believed could provide insight into the workings of the human mind. Jung is the psychiatrist and psychoanalyst who transformed the field of modern psychology.

Activity 4 consists of seven questions relating to your behaviour, actions and interactions with others. Completing it will help you identify how and where you are already embodying your calling.

Activity 5 acts to crosscheck the information you've gleaned from *Activities 1–4*. Identifying the commonalities allows you to distil and refine the themes and gives you the confidence to take the necessary steps to build a life centred around your purpose.

SHOULD I DO THE ACTIVITIES IN ORDER?

Depending on your nature, you may prefer to dive right in at *Activity 3*, so you know your life purpose straight away. However, based on my personal experience, I highly recommend you take the time and effort to look within and uncover as much information about yourself as possible through completing the other activities in this workbook.

The reason? Until you do the 'inner work' (*Activities 1, 2, 4 and 5*) to uncover the evidence of your life's calling and own what you find, you may not be ready to implement the objective opinion of someone else (*Activity 3*).

In my case, I needed to undertake an extensive journey of self-discovery before I could own the advice of life purpose specialist Narelle Duncan, which I'd received more than six years earlier! Narelle was able to clearly identify and articulate the core themes of my life calling and the role I was to play for others in this lifetime. However, it was only through completing *The Demartini Values Determination Process (Activity 1)* that I could see tangible evidence that my interests and behaviour were already aligned to my life purpose Narelle had identified.

Answering the questions that make up *Activities 2 and 4* allowed me to recognise the role I was instinctively playing with others, though I wasn't conscious of it. This helped me see that I was much closer than I realised to owning and expressing my ability to empathise with others and provide them with life-changing tools. Most importantly, it helped me recognise that there was a market for my services in a professional capacity.

Completing all five activities allowed me to build real trust in the information that I'd uncovered about myself, and the professional advice I'd received. Identifying the commonalities that arose from each activity (the aim of *Activity 5*) gave me the confidence to finally embrace my life's calling.

Similarly, those closest to me and the clients I work with have had significant breakthroughs in uncovering their reason for being and owning their life's calling by using the material I prescribe in this workbook. It is my hope that you too will receive the career inspiration you are looking for, along with a much deeper understanding of yourself. May it be life changing for you!

REQUIRED RESOURCES

Two of the activities require you to invest in some 'textbooks' and a professional service. I recommend you read through the workbook in its entirety first and take note of which activities resonate with you. Then, determine what resources you need to purchase to complete the prescribed work. Here is the full list:

Textbooks – Activity 1

1. *The Values Factor: The Secret to Creating an Inspired and Fulfilling Life* by Dr. John Demartini. (Pub: Penguin Putnam Inc; I ed; 2013) Available in print, audio and Kindle.

2. *The Artist's Way: A Spiritual Path to Higher Creativity* by Julia Cameron (Souvenir Press 2012) Available in print and Kindle.

Professional Service – Activity 2

1. Soul Purpose Astrological Analysis with Narelle Duncan at www.astrologyreading.com.au/readings.

A WORD OF ADVICE!
PLEASE READ PRIOR TO COMMENCING ANY ACTIVITIES

(Doing so will save you a lot of time, effort and money!)

Before you start the activities, it's crucial to understand **the key difference between passion and purpose**, so you don't go off on a tangent like so many others have, including myself.

Like me, you may have received the advice to 'follow your bliss' as a remedy for life's problems. Although I do believe this to be sound advice, it can prove disastrous for those who don't know the difference between passion and purpose. Both have their place in our lives, but as I mentioned earlier, I mistook a passion for my life purpose and it cost me dearly.

It can be easy to confuse a passion for your purpose, particularly if you have played it safe by conforming to societal expectations and done what is expected of you all your life. Most people know what they are passionate about (in my case – horse riding, beautiful architecture and working with my hands), but few are aware of their purpose. Fewer still are aware that you can have many passions in life but only one purpose.

Passions are tangible things for which we have unbridled enthusiasm, thoroughly enjoy doing and yearn to engage in because they give us immense pleasure and make us feel good. It's this emotional response that drives our passions. The nature of emotions and feelings, however, is that they can be fickle and change in an instant.

Your passions are extremely important because they are part of who you are, and they need to be expressed and incorporated into your daily life. However, they are not your reason for living or why you get out of bed in the morning. Building a life solely centred around your passions will not fulfil you. Instead, the role of passion is to bring happiness and joy to your daily life.

Unlike passion, which is mostly self-serving, your purpose involves being of service to others by providing solutions to their problems and adding real value to their life. It's this act of serving others that gives your life meaning and fulfilment. The aim of this workbook is to help you determine where and how you can be of service to others.

Purpose provides your life with focus, direction and meaning. Your purpose is your WHY. It's the reason you do what you do and fuels your motivation to keep going when you encounter challenges along the way. In contrast, passion gives you the impetus to start new endeavours but wanes and surrenders easily.

Speaking from personal experience, a life built solely on passion is superficial, self-indulgent and aimless. What better way to demonstrate this than through my own story? In the next section, I recount my experience and the consequences of spending more than six years chasing a passion. I also share my ensuing journey of discovering key teachers and implementing their processes. I believe seeing what an impact these processes had on my life will encourage you to try them yourself.

I hope my story inspires you, serving as an example of just what a difference knowing and living your purpose can make to your life.

FINDING MY PURPOSE

From Passion to Purpose to Joie de Vivre

When I first began the search for my life purpose, I took on board the advice of various 'experts' and began to ask myself the 'typical' questions, such as:

* What do I most love to do?

* What comes easily to me?

* What do people say I am good at?

* When am I at my best?

* What am I doing when I am at my best?

* What work do I do that doesn't seem like work?

* What experiences would I pay to have?

* What activities do I do that I never get tired or bored of?

I found answering these types of questions beneficial, to a point, because they helped me get to know myself better. However, using this process ultimately didn't yield the results or the clarity I sought. I realise now that this methodology was a scattergun approach. The outcome was a jumble of answers that lacked any real consistency or theme; my list was horse riding, wood working, interior architecture, working with my hands, helping others, making people feel better about themselves, delivering events and travelling to ancient megalithic sites.

Completing this process left me wondering if I should study architecture and interior design or become an equine therapist, which would combine my love of horses with helping people uncover behaviours that were suppressing their full potential. Or do I form a travel company that specialises in boutique tours to ancient scared megalithic sites? Which path was the correct one for me?

Unfortunately, without a definitive understanding of the themes of my life calling, I made the all too common mistake of pursuing one of my passions rather than my life purpose. It was a decision that cost me dearly, both financially and emotionally.

CHASING A PASSION

The error occurred innocently enough. I'd reached a point in my career as a Medical Imaging Technologist (aka Radiographer) where I no longer felt challenged. It was time to pursue a career that truly made my heart sing and allowed me to express my creativity.

I've always had an entrepreneurial spirit and had built a successful sideline business, making and selling suede and leather journals and cushions, which were sold in art galleries and boutique gift, book and homewares stores throughout Australia. It made sense for me to continue along a similar vein, so I began researching the homewares and interior design market, looking for ideas to expand my business.

Shortly afterwards, an opportunity arose to license an innovative technology for coating almost any item in metal. Hoping to live a life centred around the things that made me happy, I jumped at the chance to create a decorative finishes business that specialised in exquisite metal surfaces for the architectural industry.

Pursuing this path at first felt exciting and liberating. It allowed me to express my creativity, create with my hands and work alongside

Brisbane's leading interior architects and designers, without going back to university. However, as time went on and I encountered the challenges that small business owners face (franchise agreements, employing and managing staff, marketing, sales and cashflow issues, deadlines, costly manufacturing mistakes, dealing with unsatisfied customers and so on), the love for my new vocation soon wore off! Within twelve months, I was no longer jumping out of bed of a morning, eager to start my day or work on weekends.

For a little over six years, I poured all the financial resources I had into my business to keep it afloat and worked myself into the ground. The result? I not only lost my passion; I started losing my love for the industry and no longer enjoyed working with my hands.

On reflection, I now see that my decision to follow this passion was driven by a desperate need to fill a void within me, rather than a deep desire to serve others. I was trying to impress and be accepted by those whose work I admired – fuelled by my need to feel worthy. My identity was so caught up in my floundering business, I found it difficult to leave the industry even when I'd lost all passion and began to resent it.

This little detour in my life cost me dearly. I lost all confidence in myself. I no longer trusted my feelings or ability to make decisions. Every time I faced a decision, especially financial, I'd start feeling anxious. My mind would begin racing, trying to analyse the situation to determine the right choice. I often couldn't think straight and lived in perpetual fear of making the mistake of following my heart again. *I now know I'd followed a passion rather than my purpose.*

To avoid more costly mistakes and control the outcome I began a pattern of over analysing everything and consulting what I perceived to be expert business advice. However, I found that my 'logical decisions' and calculated actions often led to disastrous results. Despite my efforts, I couldn't recover my passion and ended up walking away from my business, having taken a huge financial loss.

While I'd rather forget all about this experience, in hindsight I now know it was an invaluable lesson in understanding the difference between passion and purpose, which serves today as a perfect example to help my clients and readers.

SEEKING GUIDANCE OUTSIDE

After closing my business, I needed to find a new direction. I'd tried all the avenues I knew of. The logical next step was to seek the objective opinion of a professional who specialised in career direction. Perhaps they could help me identify a financially rewarding occupation that I would also find deeply fulfilling. The obvious choice was to engage a Recruitment Agency.

After analysing my career history and answering a line of questioning similar to the list outlined above, a recruitment consultant put forward a number of suggestions based on my qualifications, previous experience and skill set. The shortlist was a number of management roles across a variety of industries. None of these appealed to me, nor did they match my industry experience.

There is no doubt that I received practical and sensible advice. However, I was not inspired. Not once did my heart skip a beat. I wasn't chomping at the bit with enthusiasm. If anything, I left the meeting feeling flat and unmotivated. I wondered if I was destined for a life of drudgery and boredom.

Despite how I felt, I took the recruiter's advice on board and kept job hunting, hoping I'd eventually find a project management role that would make my heart sing. I didn't know it at the time, but experiencing such heavy feelings in response to the specialist's recommendations was actually a sure sign I was on the wrong path.

Fortunately, sometime later I spotted a flyer for a *Soul Purpose Astrology Reading* while waiting in line at an ice-cream store. It was so out of place that it caught my attention, particularly the words 'Soul

Purpose'. I realise now that these types of external signs should not be ignored and it set me on the right path. *This topic will be explained in detail in Workbook #6.*

The flyer promised to decipher my life's calling and the lessons I was here to learn this lifetime using my birth chart, which I discovered later was primarily a blueprint of my psyche. The flyer also vowed to provide an in-depth interpretation of my personality to help me understand and integrate the different aspects of myself that were either working with or against each other, so I could fulfil my purpose in life.

Desperate to discover my reason for living, I contacted Narelle Duncan, the originator of the flyer. Two days later, I fronted up on her office doorstep, feeling nervous but excited about what our session together might reveal.

Before I continue, I'd like to clarify something. Even though Narelle uses the word 'reading' for this service, my session with her was not a psychic reading. It was an in-depth, personalised astrological analysis that went for almost two hours.

I was astonished as to the accuracy and clarity of the analysis. Not only did Narelle provide me with a general awareness and appreciation of my personality traits, her analysis was full of subtle nuances that helped me gain useful and crucial insights into myself. She described the circumstances that empowered, inspired and fulfilled me, along with those that created internal emotional tension and mental confusion when they clashed with one another. She also provided invaluable advice on how I could integrate these aspects of myself to create more inner harmony, helping to make my life journey smoother.

Another surprise was that she described the details of my birth and family dynamics prior to my conception and throughout the gestation period, as well as my relationship with my parents and the influence my family had on my development and how this had played out in my life. Using this information she could pinpoint the belief systems I had formed and how they drove my decisions and actions.

Most importantly, Narelle was able to identify and help me recognise the talents and abilities I'd been blessed with and give me clues as to the nature of my life purpose. She also revealed the lessons I was here to learn this lifetime and what others could learn from me.

I was astounded that someone, who professed to have no psychic ability and had never met me or anyone associated with me, could provide such profound personal insight using nothing more than the time, place and date of my birth. (I explain more about this process in *Activity 3*.) Having come from a scientific background (I studied Applied Science and my father was a science teacher and a self-confessed atheist), I'm naturally a sceptic of such methods. But Narelle's analysis and conclusions made me stand up and take notice.

According to Narelle, my life purpose – should I choose to accept it – was to help others heal their insecurities and build self-esteem. I'd do so by assisting them to develop confidence in their abilities and encouraging them to make self-honouring choices, rather than being influenced by others. I was to achieve this mission by disseminating information on the innovative techniques and ground-breaking resources I used to heal my own insecurities, and to build self-confidence and self-reliance at a soul level. I'd share this information in a way that people could easily understand and apply it to their own lives. Narelle predicted that my life's calling had the potential to make a global impact.

This resonated deep within me! I was excited and intrigued about what my life *could* look like. However, it also felt too good to be true. How could I successfully unlock someone's potential, heal their insecurities and build their self-esteem when I was still struggling with this myself, despite the number of books I'd read and workshops I'd attended?

So I 'parked' Narelle's analysis and chose to keep playing it safe by taking a role as a project manager, this time in the event industry.

It's a fast-paced, exciting and creative industry that allowed me to showcase my gifts and skills. This change of career was the breath of fresh air I needed at the time as it gave me the financial security I needed and the opportunity to gain new skills that would come in handy later.

Despite having a natural affinity for event management, it didn't make my heart sing. It was a frenetic industry that over time drained my energy because it was not in alignment with my life's calling. Determined to experience genuine happiness and fulfilment, I continued my search while I continued to work.

I informally explored a vast range of fields looking for a modality that would allow me to heal myself and give me the skills, knowledge and confidence to embrace my life's purpose. No stone was left unturned: psychology and personal development; meditation and yoga; natural and energy medicine; psychological astrology; metaphysics and quantum physics; as well as modalities considered by some as occult! These practices fascinated me, but they were not my calling. The more I searched, the unhappier I became.

What I was about to discover was that the answers I was looking for actually lay within.

TURNING WITHIN

It was a lecture by Dr. John Demartini on 'values' that became THE turning point in my life. His work acted as a code-breaker for discovering what was most meaningful to me and how I could contribute to the world.

As I mentioned briefly in the *Why This Workbook?* section, Dr. Demartini taught me that my 'values' are the tangible things that inspire, energise and excite me. They are the things that I am passionate about and hold in high regard. Things that I enjoy thinking about and will happily put my time, energy and money into. He helped me understand that my highest values reflect who I really am at my core. According to Dr. Demartini, my dissatisfaction with life and my chronic depression were indicative of a life out of alignment with my highest values.

The remedy for turning my life around, and the key to unlocking my life's calling, required me to identify my highest values and live in congruence with them. Inspired, I worked through Dr. Demartini's method for determining my highest values step-by-step; this involved answering thirteen questions about my core behaviours and passions.

Unlike open-ended questions such as 'What do I most love to do?', 'What activities do I participate in that I never get tired or bored of?' and 'What am I doing when I'm at my best?', Dr. Demartini's questions are relatable, real and tangible. They're effective because they focus on aspects that make up the fabric of your life – such as the objects you surround yourself with, the activities you make time for, what you spend your money on, and what you predominately think about and enjoy talking about in social settings.

Completing *The Demartini Value Determination Process* only took me a couple of hours, but I learnt critical truths about myself. It confirmed that financial security was important to me and that I was passionate about beautiful, elegant, intelligent design and expressing creativity through the use of my hands. However, passion, as I mentioned earlier, does not equal life purpose.

The consistent thread across every one of my answers to Dr. Demartini's questions was the desire to help others live their highest potential. Deep down I knew this was the main driving force behind the actions I'd taken throughout my entire life – the evidence was all around me. My home was full of self-help and psychology books. In my spare time I attended self-development seminars, workshops and retreats designed to help overcome the limitations that hold people back in life. In social settings, I'd be found in the corner deep in conversation with someone about their aspirations in life and offering ideas to support their dreams.

What a sense of relief! It was liberating to know that what I needed, what I was craving, was a life that embodied the values I identified. Completing this exercise ultimately gave me the validation, permission and confidence to begin owning the theme of my life's calling. I could now explore the things I was naturally drawn to, inspired by and valued most in life, and then build a life centred around these aspects of myself. I finally felt free to be me.

Decision making suddenly became much, much easier. It was a bit like being given a GPS after attempting to find a destination without a map. *My subsequent workbooks outline the steps I took to begin living in alignment with my life's calling and explain how I acquired the skills I needed to heal both myself and others as a by-product of doing so.*

Dr. Demartini's work on values finally allowed me to clearly comprehend the difference between passion and purpose. As a result, I recognised that my passions including interior architecture, working with my hands and horse riding needed to feature heavily in my life, but they were not my life's calling. For example, I could still honour and nurture my love for beautiful, cutting edge-design by living in an architecturally designed home built by a master craftsman and horse ride regularly, rather than making them my career.

MY LIFE NOW!

The passion I had for my metal finishes business does not compare to the love I have for the work I do now – curating content for self-transformation and empowering people to build a life they love. Don't get me wrong; I learnt a lot from taking the path that I did, the decisions I made and the experiences that resulted.

I believe everything happens for a reason, and that there is an innate intelligence guiding and directing us at all times. It creates the lessons we need to express ourselves fully and step into our life's calling. This guiding force is fervently and compassionately steering us towards the path of least resistance for completing our mission this lifetime, if only we could get out of our own way. *This topic of how we are being guided is discussed in detail in the subsequent workbooks within this series.*

Experiencing the contrast between passion and purpose led me to understand that following a passion is born primarily from a need for self-pleasure or to find identity. In contrast, purpose, which is fuelled by a genuine desire to serve others, has more humble origins. I've found that through living my purpose I'm self-fulfilled. Because I'm proud of and excited by the work I do now, I no longer need accolades and acknowledgement from others.

Living my life's calling hasn't been an easy journey or without challenges; however, I can attest that every step of the way has been enjoyable and deeply rewarding. Sure I get frustrated at times because things don't happen the way I think they should, in the timeframe that I want them to, but I've never once lost my enthusiasm or belief in what I do.

Everything else pales in comparison. It's beyond passion. This mission to help people be an authentic expression of who they are at their core is part of me. It's who I am and I feel deeply privileged and honoured to do this work. Now that I've discovered, and am living my purpose, there is no turning back.

It's this sort of focus and exuberance that makes the impossible possible and has the capacity to create real change in the world. This verve also exists within you and when unleashed will alter your experience of life, profoundly and irrevocably.

To ensure your journey isn't as long or arduous as mine, I recommend you complete all the activities set out in this workbook. If your answers are consistent across *Activities 1–4*, the themes of your life calling resonates deeply within you and the thought of living this purpose would be a dream come true, you've struck gold. I'd strongly encourage you to follow this rich seam all the way.

Enough said. It's now time for you to do some work. Are you ready to discover the themes of your life's purpose?

TIME TO TAKE ACTION: UNCOVER THE THEME OF YOUR LIFE PURPOSE

I believe, like many of the great spiritual teachers I admire, that each of us is born with a unique purpose that is essential to the wellbeing of others and the greater good of the planet. Our role this lifetime is to discover and fully embrace our purpose, along with our innate (and often unrecognised) gifts and talents. The reward, for those courageous individuals who take on this role, is a life filled with meaning, fulfilment and joy.

The even better news? Your life purpose is a unique combination of skills, abilities, qualities and attributes that allows you to provide a service to others in a way that only you can, and gain the financial support you need. Living your life purpose won't feel like work. It's something you would do for free because it brings you such immense satisfaction.

Now, all you have to do is uncover it. That information is already inside of you, and the key to finding it is in knowing exactly what questions to ask yourself and where to look.

This section of the book is about taking action. Reading about the activities is not the same as completing them. The processes and services I prescribe are powerful and will change the course of your life, if you are willing to take the time and effort to do the work. The journey of self-discovery strips away who you are not, so you can finally free to be your authentic self across every aspect of your life.

I highly recommend writing all your epiphanies, insights and answers into the space provided. Your responses will point to aspects or themes of your life's calling and ultimately help to build a clear picture of your life purpose.

It doesn't matter in which order you do the activities. What is most important is that you do them. Ideally, you'd complete them all regardless of how long it takes. Doing so will lead to a much deeper and more intimate relationship with yourself and ultimately make navigating life so much easier. I found the first activity was critical so I recommend you start there.

I encourage you not to be daunted by the amount of work each activity appears to entail. It will be much more fun than you think. After all, the self-discovery process is all about you and getting to know you. So have fun with it and enjoy the process. You might be pleasantly surprised by what you discover.

Reminder: If you haven't read through the whole workbook yet, you may want to glance over all of the activities to get a sense of the territory we will be covering and to purchase the required resources.

DOWNLOAD YOUR FREE ANSWER SHEET

If you are like me and prefer to keep your books pristine, you can download the FREE *Workbook #1 Answer Sheet*. This document has been created for recording and processing your responses and will help you to gain a clear picture of your overall WHY in life:

www.aguideforlife.com/downloads/workbook-1-answer-sheet

ACTIVITY 1:
DETERMINING YOUR VALUES

"The space and time in your innermost dominant thought determines your outermost tangible reality."

~ Dr. John Demartini

REQUIRED RESOURCE: Chapter 2 of *The Values Factor: The Secret to Creating an Inspired and Fulfilling Life* by Dr. John Demartini. (Pub: Penguin Putnam Inc; 1 ed; 2013) Available in print, audio and Kindle. Or access *The Demartini Values Determination Process* online for free via his website: https://drdemartini.com/values/login.

Based on my experience, *The Demartini Values Determination Process* is the best method for truly getting to know who you are at your core by determining your highest values and their hierarchy of order. According to Dr. Demartini, the hierarchy of your values determines 'what you perceive' and 'how you act' in life, which subsequently governs 'your immediate destiny'. He believes that as your values changes, so too does your destiny. Hence, finding your unchanging core values deep within you, rather than being influenced by your passions, is key to indentifying your life purpose.

I recommend this activity for *everyone*. As described in the *Finding My Purpose* section, Dr. Demartini's process helped me to not only recognise what I valued in life, but more importantly what I valued the most. The questions are relatable and easy to complete. Finding the answers within yourself is a very powerful process as it helps you recognise that you already possess the qualities, talents and skills for living and fulfilling your life purpose. It's no surprise then that Dr. Demartini's motto for this process is 'Know yourself. Be yourself'.

To complete this exercise, you will need to either purchase a copy of his book *The Values Factor: The Secret to Creating an Inspired and Fulfilling Life* or access the online version of *The Demartini Values Determination Process* (the link for which is shared above). Although the online version is free, you will need to create an account by providing your name and e-mail address. If you are happy to receive correspondence from Dr. John Demartini and don't want to spend any money, this option may be best.

If you choose to purchase a copy of *The Values Factor* for this activity, you will be working with *Chapter 2 – Identifying Your Values*. While an audiobook is also available, you might find that reading written instructions is easier than listening to them when completing this type of exercise.

If you are an avid reader and book lover like me, you might enjoy reading *The Values Factor* regardless of what format you use to complete this exercise. It is Dr. Demartini's most comprehensive work to date on his concept of values. He includes examples of how historical geniuses achieved greatness though living in accordance with their values and offers methods on how to integrate these notions into your life.

ACTIVITY 1

Before you start this exercise, retreat and switch off from the outside world.

Step 1: Self-exploration to determine your hierarchy of values

Take your time and answer the thirteen questions that make up *The Demartini Values Determination Process*, as honestly and thoughtfully as you can, following the instructions step by step. Record your answers in the space provided below, rather than in *The Values Factor* book or online, as you will need to compare your answers with the information gleaned from completing the remaining workbook activities.

QUESTION I: Personal space

1. _____

   _____

   _____

2. _____

   _____

   _____

3. _____

   _____

   _____

QUESTION 2: Personal time

1. _____

_____

_____

2. _____

_____

_____

3. _____

_____

_____

QUESTION 3: Energy

1. _____

_____

_____

2. _____

_____

_____

3. _____

_____

_____

QUESTION 4: Money

1. _____

_____

_____

2. _____

_____

_____

3. _____

_____

_____

QUESTION 5: Order and organisation

1. _____

_____

_____

2. _____

_____

_____

3. _____

_____

_____

QUESTION 6: Reliability, discipline and focus

1. _____

_____

_____

2. _____

_____

_____

3. _____

_____

_____

QUESTION 7: Thoughts

1. _____

_____

_____

2. _____

_____

_____

3. _____

_____

_____

QUESTION 8: Visualisation

1. _____

_____

2. _____

_____

3. _____

_____

QUESTION 9: Inner dialogue

1. _____

_____

2. _____

_____

3. _____

_____

QUESTION 10: Social settings

1. _____

_____

2. _____

_____

3. _____

_____

QUESTION 11: Inspiration

1. _____
   _____
   _____

2. _____
   _____
   _____

3. _____
   _____
   _____

QUESTION 12: Long-term goals

1. _____
   _____
   _____

2. _____
   _____
   _____

3. _____
   _____
   _____

QUESTION 13: Learning

1. _____
   _____
   _____

2. _____
   _____
   _____

3. _____
   _____
   _____

Step 2: **Rank your answers to find your highest values**

Now that you have answered the thirteen questions, use different coloured highlighters to identify the answers that repeat most often, following the instructions provided by Dr. Demartini. Then rank them below, starting with the answer that appears most frequently. *Note: I recommend you assign one colour to each theme that arises, and remain consistent with your choice and assignment of colours across all the activities. You may not require all the lines listed below. Use as many as you need and add more if necessary.*

1. _____

2. _____

3. _____

4. _____

5. _____

6. _____

7. _____

8. _____

9. _____

10. _____

How did you go?

Did a common theme emerge? Can you see a recurrent thread of behaviours and passions running through your answers to all thirteen questions, or at least the majority? This common thread or theme gives an indication of your highest values.

If the pattern that emerged is clear, I suggest you move on to *Activity 2*. If there was no real consistency in your answers, or you found it difficult to answer any or all of the questions, please do not despair. It simply means that you do not know yourself well enough yet, and you're not alone in that! I can assure you that once you have developed a deeper understanding of yourself, the theme of your life's purpose will emerge with crystal clarity if you repeat Dr. Demartini's process. To assist you, directly below is a powerful self-discovery resource that I (and millions of others) have found extremely valuable.

Getting to know yourself

To assist you in developing an intimate relationship with yourself, I highly recommend you work through Julia Cameron's book, *The Artist's Way: A Spiritual Path to Higher Creativity*. Doing so will take you on a 12-week journey of self-discovery. *The Artist's Way* contains hundreds of extremely effective practical exercises, many of which are designed to help you explore who you really are and what inspires you.

I personally found that answering questions like – 'If you had five other lives to lead, what would you do in each of them?', 'What are twenty things you enjoy doing?', 'Who are five people you admire?' and 'What traits do these people have?' – challenged and opened me up to think in new and more creative ways.

The Artist's Way helped me form a deeper understanding of myself. In fact, it laid the groundwork for being able to quickly and successfully complete Dr. Demartini's method for determining my highest values.

Once you've completed *The Artist's Way*, repeat *Activity I.*

ACTIVITY 2:
WHO DO YOU ASPIRE TO BE?

*"Don't dance around the perimeter of the
person you want to be."*

~ Gabrielle Bernstein

Now that you have completed the *Demartini Values Determination
Process* and given voice to what you value most in life, below are
some additional questions to reveal more about your true nature.

These questions are a compilation and extrapolation of more
commonly asked 'life purpose questions'. They helped me to clarify
the types of activities and fields that inspired me and who I aspired
to be in life.

Also I have found these questions to be powerful catalysts in a
clinical setting. They've assisted my clients to discover more about
their passions, what they deeply desire and the type of person they
hope to be.

*Note: Underneath each question are my answers, so you can see
how they relate to my life purpose.*

ACTIVITY 2

Before you start this activity, retreat and switch off from the outside world.

Step 1: Questions and answers

Take your time and answer the five questions below as honestly and thoughtfully as you can.

QUESTION I: If money, time, logistics, level of experience and talent weren't an issue, what field of study would you enrol in or activities would you participate in – just for fun?

EXAMPLE: I would spend all my time researching why people often don't fulfil their potential and studying the qualities possessed by those that do. I would also study neuroscience and quantum physics to understand more about the mind-body connection and how to overcome the mental barriers that prevent people from being the best versions of themselves and living a fulfilling and joyous life.

QUESTION 2: If money, time and logistics weren't an issue, what occupation or activity would you happily volunteer to do indefinitely or pay money to participate in – purely to be part of the experience or to gain personal wisdom?

EXAMPLE: I would pay to attend the events and workshops of the world's leading self-transformation teachers, so that I could become more confident within myself, communicate my needs, express myself fully, and be more present and content in the moment. With this newfound wisdom, I would dedicate my life to assisting others to transform theirs. I would also volunteer to work in the offices of the world's leading neuroscientists, brain training specialists, human behaviour experts, and integrative and functional medicine facilities, to learn about cutting-edge brain science and mind-body medicine. I would apply the knowledge gained to be the best possible version of myself and assist others to do the same.

QUESTION 3: If you had so much money that you no longer had to work to earn a living and you had all the time and support you needed, what is the one problem you'd like to solve?

EXAMPLE: For as long as I can remember I've been fascinated by people – mesmerised by their magnificence and awed by their innate talent. The problem I want to solve is why not everyone fulfils their potential, and how it can be unlocked and activated. Specifically, what has puzzled me most is why some of the most gifted people I know either keep their brilliance hidden from the world at large or struggle to become recognised in a career that expresses their forte. What I find even more baffling and frustrating is why others, whose skills, flair and aptitude are inferior to their peers, achieve fame and fortune.

QUESTION 4: Who do you aspire to be and why? Is there one person dead or alive that embodies the qualities and characteristics you aim to emulate?

EXAMPLE: The person I chose is Alana Fairchild, my spiritual teacher. She has the incredible gift of intuitively recognising and articulating what your soul wants to express in this lifetime. She can also sense which aspects of your human self are blocking your soul's yearning for expression. She then provides personalised feedback and practical examples to help you get out of your own way and express yourself fully in the world. She performs this role without judgement and in a way that you can understand and relate to. Her manner is kind, loving and compassionate.

QUESTION 5: Is there one invaluable piece of wisdom or skill that you wish you'd learnt early in life? It could be something that made a profound and positive impact on a challenging aspect of your life.

EXAMPLE: Learning about the power of the subconscious mind changed my life. I wish I had been taught as a child the role my thoughts, words, feelings and actions play in the manifestation process, and how to reprogram my subconscious mind.

Step 2: **Rank your answers**

Now that you have answered the five questions, use different coloured highlighters to identify the answers that repeat most often and rank them below, starting with the answer that appears most frequently. *Note: I recommend you assign one colour to each theme that arises, and remain consistent with your choice and assignment of colours across all the activities. You may not require all the lines listed below. Use as many as you need.*

1. _____

2. _____

3. _____

4. _____

5. _____

6. _____

7. _____

8. _____

9. _____

10. _____

Completing this activity helped me realise that what I desired most was to make a real difference in people's lives, by helping them to: gain the self-confidence to fully express their talents and abilities; overcome their self-sabotaging behaviours, limiting beliefs and emotional baggage that is holding them back in life; and experience real joy and happiness (which is what I was desperately craving myself!). I aspired to have the skills, knowledge, ability, wisdom and compassion to unlock the potential in others (and myself) and give them the freedom to be the best possible version of themselves.

How did you go?

Did some common themes emerge from completing this activity? Is there a recurrent thread of desires and aspirations running through your answers to these questions that matches your highest values, as identified in *Activity I*.

If no clear theme emerged or you found it difficult to answer any of the questions, it simply means that you do not know yourself well enough yet. As suggested above, I recommend you work through Julia Cameron's book, *The Artist's Way: A Spiritual Path to Higher Creativity*.

If the pattern that emerged is clear and you would like to dive deeper into what you've discovered and learn more about the theme of your life's calling, I'd suggest you move on to *Activity 3*. A session with career specialist and counsellor, Narelle Duncan, will pinpoint a very concise direction, and, let's face it, sometimes we need to hear the same thing from multiple sources until it really sinks in!

Alternatively, you could move on to *Activity 4*. This will evoke insight into how you are already demonstrating the themes of your life's calling day to day. That being said, from my experience, I would suggest you still do *Activity 3*. As I found, even if you gain clarity on your highest values, you still risk following a passion instead of your purpose.

ACTIVITY 3:
LIFE PURPOSE ASTROLOGICAL ANALYSIS

"Obviously astrology has much to offer psychology, but what the latter can offer its elder sister is less evident."

~ Carl G. Jung

REQUIRED RESOURCE: Schedule a Soul Purpose Astrological Analysis with Narelle Duncan www.astrologyreading.com.au.

Seeking an objective opinion about career direction and life purpose from a professional astrologer might sound esoteric, wacky, kooky, weird or downright wrong, and in the past I would have concurred. However, I'm yet to find another modality that can compete with the detail, depth and accuracy of the personality and behavioural profile Narelle Duncan provides during a consultation.

Prior to my astrological analysis with Narelle I'd completed several types of assessments trying to achieve the same level of personal profiling, as exemplified in the following list. You might recognise some of these or even have completed them as a way of finding out more about yourself:

- Myers-Briggs Type Indicator (MBTI)
- IQ Test
- Herrmann Brain Dominance Instrument (HBDI)
- The 5 Love Languages Profile
- Dharma Type
- Human Design
- Jung Typology Test
- Kolbe A Index
- Passion Test
- Personal Values Assessment
- Riso-Hudson Enneagram Type Indicator
- The Four Tendencies Quiz
- VIA Survey.

Even though they designed to assess your personality profile and type, thinking preferences, how smart you are, your instinctive way of doing things, your strengths, passions and values, I found the multiple choice line of questioning and the computer generated report with this style of assessments impersonal. In most instances I related to two or three answers per question, but found it difficult to select just one as the most accurate for definitively encapsulating me. Also, my selection varied depending on my mood and life stage. For this reason, tests and quizzes like these make me feel like a square peg being rammed into a round hole.

My consultation with Narelle was the exact opposite, and it took me completely by surprise. Her astrological analysis provided a personalised and strikingly accurate interpretation of my personality, interests, abilities and the way I experience life. It also revealed subtle nuances that helped me gain useful and crucial insights about myself, including highly individualised aspects and traits that rang true, but that I had not yet consciously acknowledged.

I've since referred family, friends, associates, work colleagues and clients to Narelle and they report equally valuable outcomes. My hope is that you will too. Most importantly, it's the quickest way to acquire laser-sharp insight into your life's calling.

How does astrology work and what can I gain?

Swiss psychiatrist and psychoanalyst, Carl Gustav Jung, who founded analytical psychology and transformed the field of modern psychology, believed that astrology could provide insight into the workings of the human mind. Having studied astrology myself, I now firmly believe that it provides not only an extremely accurate and reliable system for discovering your reason for living, but also valuable insight into the self-sabotaging patterns and limiting beliefs that are holding you back from fulfilling your dreams.

One of my astrology teachers, Maggie Kerr, taught me that astrology offers a model for the human psyche. The position of the 'planets' at the precise moment of our birth, she says, creates a resonance or imprint that shapes our persona and influences our potential. This notion is similar to the way the Moon's gravitational pull on the Earth's surface affects ocean tides and how its phases coincide with biological rhythms in animal, plant and human life. Similarly, the Sun's position relative to Earth determines seasonal cycles that influence circadian rhythms, mood and behaviour patterns of living organisms. Not to mention how other celestial bodies affect Earth and its inhabitants.

Your Natal Chart (birth chart) depicts an astrological snapshot of the sky at the precise moment you were born and is calculated from the date, time and place of your birth. A stylised circular chart maps out the location of around twelve celestial bodies (sometimes slightly more or slightly less depending on the training and preference of the astrologer) in a symbolic language that provides a 'blueprint' of your psyche. Using this chart, a professional astrologer can ascertain who you are at your very core, your deepest desires and the nature of your full potential, devoid of cultural influences, societal expectations, the opinion of others and your self-limiting beliefs, doubts and fears. In a nutshell, a personalised astrological analysis gets to the heart of the matter quickly, regardless of the extent of your self-exploration.

The time of birth is particularly crucial. It is this, Maggie says, that 'individualises' the chart, pinpointing a person's 'energetic imprint'. For instance, the mechanics of astrology reveals subtle variations in the birth chart of twins born within minutes of each other. This assists an astrologer to ascertain their individual personality traits and potential.

A Natal Chart can provide the following insights, when interpreted by a professional astrologer:

- the influences at the time of your conception and throughout the gestation period, as well as the conditions of your birth and the dynamics between your parents during the pregnancy and at your birth

- the family environment you were born into and whether this created a sense of safety and security

- the characteristics and belief systems of your parents and how these factors influenced your development

- your natural gifts, skills and talents and whether these are easily expressed, along with how your reasoning, comprehension and learning style may be used as a tool for growth and development

- the nature of difficulties and challenges you are likely to face throughout your life

- the way you relate to others and the type of partners you will be attracted to

- the work or career that will give you the most satisfaction and be of service to others

- your psycho-emotional beliefs and how they affect your wellbeing and health

- the nature of your spiritual and religious persuasions, and how these beliefs, or lack of them, are instrumental in you finding a sense of meaning and purpose in life

- the children you may bear and the ongoing themes and issues you may play out with them.

(Ref: Kerr, M. *Universal Astrology: An in depth course in astrology aligning the four aspects of wholeness – spiritual, psychological, emotional, physical (Workbook One)*, Universal Astrology, Southport, 1999.)

The quality and accuracy of your astrological analysis is subject to the precision of your birth data and its interpretation by your astrologer, depending on their skills, experience and the type of astrology they practise. Hence, it's important to find the right astrologer.

That is why I recommend the work of Narelle Duncan. She assisted me to know my life purpose and presented invaluable insights on many of the points mentioned above. Specifically, Narelle helped me better understand the different aspects of myself and how to integrate them harmoniously, the influences from my childhood and the beliefs and thought processes I'd created as a result, the lessons I am here to learn... and so much more!

The information that you will glean from *Activity 3* will also be extremely beneficial in subsequent workbooks – where you begin to identify and remove any obstacles, particularly self-sabotaging patterns, preventing you from expressing yourself fully, achieving your goals and living your life's calling.

If at this point you've decided that *Activity 3* isn't for you, I under-stand. If this is the choice you have made, I recommend that you complete *Activities 1, 2, 4 and 5* to ensure you have discovered as much information about yourself and the themes of your purpose prior to making any major changes to your life. Otherwise, enjoy your consultation with Narelle.

ACTIVITY 3

Step 1: **Obtain your birth data**

You will need to provide your astrologer with your birth details including:

* date of birth
* location of birth
* precise time of birth.

If the time of your birth is out, even by a few minutes, this will affect the accuracy of your astrological analysis. If you don't know the time of your birth, I'd recommend you check your birth certificate, ask relatives or contact the records department of the hospital where you were born. If you have exhausted all these channels, a professional astrologer can do a process called 'rectification' to determine your birth time. This is an additional service, and because of the time involved, it can be the same price as your astrology consultation.

If you do engage your astrologer to calculate your birth time, you will often need to provide them with the dates of at least ten important events that occurred in your life, along with a brief description of each event and how you felt at the time. In this instance the month and year of the event will suffice. Examples of significant life events include: the birth of a child; death of a parent, sibling, partner or child; marriage; divorce; house moves or relocations to another city, state or country; and major travel.

Step 2: **Choose a professional astrologer**

Narelle Duncan is not the only professional astrologer who offers an astrological analysis to determine your life purpose. She is, however, someone whom I trust implicitly and highly recommend. Her consultations are conducted in person at her practice in Burleigh Heads, Queensland, Australia or via phone or Skype for interstate and international clients.

If you live outside of the South East Queensland region and would prefer to work with an astrologer who is a little closer to home, choose one who holds a recognised qualification (issued by an internationally accepted astrology association) and specialises in soul-centred, modern, psychologically-based astrology. They also need to be able to synthesise your chart to extract the key archetypes and soul messages, and then create practical and relatable everyday life examples. *Note: A traditional, Vedic or personality-focused astrologer will not provide you with the same level of detail and accuracy on your life's purpose as the type of astrologer mentioned above.*

Step 3: **Choose the type of session and schedule it**

Narelle offers two types of soul purpose astrological analysis sessions:

- 1-hour Soul Purpose Astrology Reading
- 1.5-hour Soul Purpose Astrology Reading + Future Forecast.

The Future Forecast component of the consultation will provide insight into potential opportunities and experiences that will influence the next 12 months of your life. Being privy to this information will help you identify the aspects of your life that are being affected during this period and assist you in the choices you make. It will also help you understand when to take action and when to hold back.

Narelle can be contacted for a consultation by calling:
+6I 7 5576 3422.
You can also book your session on-line using the following link:
www.astrologyreading.com.au/readings

Step 4: **Record the session**

Make sure your consultation is recorded as you will need to refer to it later. If your astrologer does not provide you with a recording of your session or won't permit you to record it, you will need to take detailed notes throughout your consultation. If this is something that you are not good at, or you'd rather focus on the session, ask a friend or family member to act as a scribe for you. *Note: Narelle records her consultations and will provide you with a MP3 file via e-mail following your session.*

Step 5: **Analyse your consultation notes**

Go back and listen to the recording and take detailed notes or reread the notes that were taken during your session. When doing so, take particular notice of the following things your astrologer indicated about you:

- the theme of your life purpose
- the lessons you are here to learn and teach others
- any unique traits, qualities and skills
- what you love
- what you value

- the career paths you could consider
- core unconscious beliefs
- particular circumstances and challenges that create inner tension and cause you to lose power, become indecisive or compromise your needs.

Step 6: **Write your themes and lessons**

When you have finished taking notes, summarise in the space below:

- the theme(s) of your life purpose

_____

_____

_____

_____

_____

- the lessons you are here to learn and teach others.

_____

_____

_____

_____

_____

Step 7: **Journal your feelings**

Now that you have completed this activity, take a moment to notice how you are feeling and use the space below to describe the emotions you are experiencing. This will be useful to refer to or reflect on at a later time.

How you feel is key to discerning if you are on the right path. As mentioned in the *Finding My Purpose* section, when I engaged the professional services of a Recruitment Agency to help me determine the role I was best suited for, their recommendations did not inspire or excite me at all. I felt the opposite. Dread! I now know that I should have acknowledged those feelings and paused.

If your astrologer has done a good job, deep down you should be feeling extremely excited, even if at this point your life's purpose might seem too good to be true or you are feeling a little overwhelmed, not knowing where to begin. Don't panic! I will address any concerns you might have in the *Conclusion* section of this workbook.

I know what it feels like to tap into your life purpose, and I've seen the reactions of my clients and loved ones when they identify their reason for living. Their eyes light up and they break into a big grin! It's as if a wellspring of light and excitement erupts from within and they can't help expressing it.

When you've tapped into your life purpose it's palpable. It's what I imagine it would feel like to strike gold or win the lottery, only better. Discovering your calling gives you a reason for living.

ACTIVITY 4:
OWNING YOUR PURPOSE

"There is no greater gift you can receive than to honour your calling. It's why you were born. And how you become most truly alive."

~ Oprah Winfrey

You have explored your core values and who you desire to be. Your *Soul Purpose Astrological Analysis* will have helped you also understand yourself more and pinpointed the themes of your life purpose. Through these steps you're getting closer to uncovering your life's calling! Now it's time to gain even deeper insight into where you are already innately demonstrating and enacting those themes every day.

The questions in this activity aim to distinguish your natural gifts and talents from the ones you've acquired to survive the environment you were born into. For example, despite feeling depleted both emotionally and energetically at the end of each workday, I found it extremely difficult to move on from financially lucrative employment for which I was in high demand. Working through these questions helped to eliminate my fears and finally step into my purpose.

The questions that make up this activity have evolved from more commonly asked 'life purpose questions.' My clients and those closest to me have found these questions to be powerful in truly owning their life's calling.

Note: Underneath each question are my answers, so you can see how they relate to my life purpose.

ACTIVITY 4

Before you start this activity, retreat and switch off from the outside world.

Step 1: **Questions and answers**

Take your time and answer the seven questions below, as honestly and thoughtfully as you can.

QUESTION I: What have you always done in every job you have ever had that has nothing to do with the role you were employed to do?

This question was given to my friend Paul Fry by Career Coach, Lucy Dodd.

EXAMPLE: I could instantly see how I had played the informal role of workplace counsellor throughout my career history, as well as at school and university. People naturally come to me with their problems. I listen to them, empathise with them, make them feel better about themselves, and encourage them to take actions that will serve and empower them. This is a key component of my life's calling.

QUESTION 2: What day-to-day act of service do you naturally provide for others simply because doing so gives you great pleasure and you find it easy to do? It might be something that they appreciate, enjoy or gain benefit from.

EXAMPLE: People naturally gravitate to and share their problems with me. I enjoy empowering them by making them feel better about themselves and their situation simply by listening to and empathising with them. Where appropriate, I offer them a new perspective on their circumstances and direct them to relevant resources and tools. What I love most is pointing out their natural abilities and talents and encouraging them to find ways to express themselves more fully.

QUESTION 3: Do you have an innate skill, strength or quality that comes so naturally and easily to you that you don't realise others can't do it to the same level as you?

This talent might not be obvious to you at first as it is simply part of who you naturally are. For instance, if you become frustrated with others because they can't see what is blindingly obvious to you, or they can't do something to your standard, it might be a clue that you have a special gift in that area. Often it takes someone close to you to point out that not everyone has this ability.

EXAMPLE: My ability to make people feel good about themselves was pointed out to me recently by a couple of friends, who are also travelling companions. Although both of these people know one another, they are not close, yet individually they shared insights on how quickly and easily I was able to make genuine connections with fellow travellers and commented on the positive impact I made on the people I interacted with. I was quite taken aback by their comments as it wasn't something I was consciously aware of doing.

Shortly afterwards, I began to recall situations during my school days and throughout my employment history where classmates or employers gave me the role of 'smoothing the waters' whenever a conflict arose with another student or work colleague. They believed I always knew the right thing to say that would make the other person feel better and disarm the situation.

I get along with pretty much anyone and I'm often perplexed and frustrated when others don't make the same effort. This is particularly noticeable in situations that require people to put their judgments and differences aside to connect and achieve an outcome that will benefit all parties involved.

QUESTION 4: Is there a role that you regularly perform for strangers that you don't intentionally orchestrate?

Such instances often provide insight into your destined role in life.

EXAMPLE: Regardless of where I go, I am regularly stopped in the street by strangers who need guidance or help with directions. I'm also often the first port of call with friends, family and associates looking for advice on who to contact or where to go for all sorts of information.

QUESTION 5: Do people who you barely know or have just met entrust you with their deepest, darkest secrets or share information with you that would normally be difficult to come by? If so, write down any kinds of scenarios that have occurred and make notes on the type of unusual information and secrets people share with you and/or the particular advice they are seeking.

This will often give you further insight into your life's purpose.

EXAMPLE: People who I have just met often pour their heart out to me. For some reason they feel safe enough to tell me all their most intimate problems, fears and insecurities. They share information with me that they wouldn't ever dare tell their partner, family or friends.

QUESTION 6: Is there an action that is impossible for you not to do? In other words, is there something in work or in everyday life you can't help doing because you feel it makes a real difference?

Scott Dinsmore, founder of Live Your Legend (a career and connection platform to inspire people to find their passion) asks individuals to ponder this question in order to determine their life purpose.

EXAMPLE: It doesn't matter where I go or what I do, I can't help but assist people who are lost and need direction. Whether that be a stranger on the street looking for directions or people who come to me with their problems. I feel compelled to point them in the right direction. I do so by providing them with information based my knowledge and personal experience or by directing them to the appropriate person or resources that will provide them with the correct information and support.

Also, throughout my career I've taken it upon myself to create procedure manuals whenever they haven't existed in a workplace, particularly where staff are required to perform complex processes.

QUESTION 7: What activity or work do you love so much that you: become so preoccupied that you lose all track of time and space; information or knowledge comes to mind easily; and everything seems to flow and fall into place? When you finish the activity you genuinely feel good about yourself and as if you have really accomplished something great. You look forward to doing it again.

EXAMPLE: I find that when I'm fully present and engaged in listening whenever someone is telling me their problems and are open to receiving my wisdom, time seems to speed up. I'm also able to recall facts and information that I wouldn't normally. My mind sharpens and I become more articulate than usual. I genuinely leave these sorts of interactions feeling emotionally buoyant and aware that I have made a difference in someone else's life.

_____

_____

_____

_____

_____

_____

_____

_____

_____

_____

_____

_____

Step 2: **Rank your answers**

Now that you have answered the seven questions, use different coloured highlighters to identify the answers that repeat most often and rank them below, starting with the answer that appears most frequently. *Note: I recommend you assign one colour to each theme that arises, and remain consistent with your choice and assignment of colours across all the activities. You may not require all the lines listed below. Use as many as you need.*

1. _____

2. _____

3. _____

4. _____

5. _____

6. _____

7. _____

8. _____

9. _____

10. _____

How did you go?

Are you beginning to see where you are already fulfilling your purpose? After I completed this activity, it became really obvious that people, particularly those who felt lost and directionless in life, were very drawn to me. They were seeking comfort and looking for advice and direction on to how to solve their life's problems. I began to see that I already had the skills, ability and compassion to make a real difference in people's lives. I also noticed I felt a sense of achievement and was more emotionally uplifted whenever I could provide someone with information, knowledge or wisdom that they found helpful. How do you feel knowing that in some areas of your life you are already expressing your purpose?

ACTIVITY 5:
DISTILLING THE THEMES OF YOUR LIFE PURPOSE

"We are not on this earth to accumulate victories or trophies but to be whittled down until what is felt is who we truly are."

~ Arianna Huffington

Each activity so far has revealed more about yourself – what you value, who you aspire to be, the themes of your life purpose and where you are already expressing your calling in daily life. Now that you have completed *Activities 1–4*, it's time to review your answers across the board to identify the common threads. As you review each of the activity summations, use the space below to jot down any commonalities. The aim is to collate an all-encompassing and clearer picture of the themes of your life purpose.

ACTIVITY 5

Before you start this activity, retreat and switch off from the outside world.

Step 1: **Common themes**

1. Write down any common themes that emerged from Activity 1.

_____

_____

_____

_____

_____

_____

_____

_____

2: Write down any common themes that emerged from Activity 2.

_____

_____

_____

_____

_____

_____

_____

_____

_____

3: Write down any common themes that emerged from Activity 3.

_____

_____

_____

_____

_____

_____

_____

4: Write down any common themes that emerged from Activity 4.

_____

_____

_____

_____

_____

_____

_____

Does a clear pattern emerge? Or are some of the spaces above left blank because your answers are conflicting or diverse? If there is diversity amongst your answers to *Activities 1–4*, I suggest you review each, one at a time, and take particular notice of how you feel when you think about what you have discovered. Then move onto *Step 2*.

Step 2: Summarise the themes of your life purpose

You will know you are on the right track if you can identify a clear theme across all of your answers in Step I above. If this is the case, to the best of your ability summarise the themes of your life purpose, along with where you can already see these playing out in your life.

How did you go?

How are you feeling about what you have uncovered? If any of your answers excite, inspire or uplift you, it is a clear indication you are heading in the right direction. A word of caution – if the theme identified is an activity that you love doing, but that is largely *self-serving*, there is a strong possibility you have uncovered a *passion rather than a purpose*. Remember, *purpose involves being of service to others*. Don't worry though; it's just a sign of a bit more work to do.

On the other hand, if the theme you've identified provides solutions for others and adds real value to their life, congratulations! You are definitely on the right track, even if you might not exactly know how you are going to go about it just yet or what your life could look like when you are living your calling.

If this is where you find yourself, the subsequent workbooks will guide you through the appropriate course of action needed to initiate and activate you living your purpose. What's important at this point is how you feel now that you've discovered the themes of your calling.

If you feel indifferent or less than enthusiastic about any of the answers you gleaned from working through this process, it could indicate that you have more work to do on building an intimate relationship with yourself, or the birth data used might not be accurate. As mentioned earlier, providing your astrologer with the precise time, date and location of your birth is imperative. In particular, a birth time that is out even by a few minutes can affect the accuracy of your astrological analysis.

As we continue our work together, you'll discover that your feelings not only act as an inner GPS to guide you in the right direction, but they also play a valuable role in activating and magnetically drawing in the experiences and people you require to live your purpose. This might be too much to comprehend at this stage. Be rest-assured the role emotions play in our lives and the manifesting process will be covered in detail in the second workbook within this series.

For now, congratulate yourself on completing the self-discovery tasks assigned. You've taken the first crucial step in building a life you love. It's a huge accomplishment and you deserve to celebrate and bask in this achievement. Very few people ever really get to know themselves and assess what they truly need and desire. As a consequence they unknowingly settle for a mediocre life instead of one that is deeply fulfilling, overflowing with joy and inspiring to others.

CONCLUSION

Now that you've completed this workbook you will either have a crystal-clear understanding of the themes of your life purpose or you will need to do some further self-exploration to uncover and own it fully.

If your reason for living isn't clear right now, do not despair. I recommend that you dive deeply into Julia Cameron's book *The Artist's Way*, the *Inspirational Resources* section at the back of this workbook and any other self-discovery material you can get your hands on. Once you've uncovered more about yourself, repeat *Activities 1, 2, 4 and 5* and the themes of your life's calling will crystallise. Most importantly, enjoy every step of the self-discovery process.

In the meantime, there are plenty of other steps you can take in preparing to embody your life's calling such as eliminating any self-limiting beliefs or emotional baggage that might prevent you from expressing yourself fully in the future. I would encourage you to continue to familiarise yourself with the material featured on the aguideforlife.com website, particularly Chapters 3 and 4 under the *My Story* section of the site. It's a free resource that will also set you in good stead for completing the rest of the workbooks in this series.

On the other hand, if you have struck gold and are now crystal clear about the theme of your life purpose, I'm guessing you are doing one of two things: chomping at the bit to begin living in accordance with your life's calling or thinking that it seems far too good to be true.

If you are excited and can't wait to get started, your mind is probably racing with all sorts of possibilities and new ideas. Don't go charging ahead just yet as there is some key information you need to know before you start making radical changes to your life. I've made that mistake, several times, and it didn't end well.

Instead, I encourage you to work methodically through the series of workbooks I've created to help you build a life you love. The reason? You've still got a lot more to learn about what is needed to successfully live your life's purpose. I assure you, being armed with the powerful knowledge I have to share will save you a lot of time, effort, money and heartache. It's vital you lay strong foundations that will set you up and support you to have positive experiences, rather than painful ones.

Now that you've identified your life's calling, the next stage involves reshaping your life so that every aspect of it – your focus, your intentions, your goals, your actions, your relationships, your career, your lifestyle and most importantly your subconscious beliefs – are in alignment with the themes of your purpose. By doing so, you'll become a magnet for opportunities that allow you to easily and effortlessly live your purpose.

Remember, you already possess the natural abilities and qualities required to express yourself fully and embody your reason for living, though you may need to hone them a little. Even the most gifted athletes and musicians still have to train, practise and rehearse.

If you have clearly identified the themes of your life purpose but are feeling one or all of the following: somewhat apprehensive and wondering how you could possibly make a career out of doing something that you love; overwhelmed and not sure where to begin; and you can't picture yourself living your life purpose... don't panic! You are now ready for the next stage in building a life you love and deserve with *Workbook #2*. This next step will help you create a clear and realistic vision of what your life could look like.

Personalised support

I understand that the journey of self-discovery and the process of change can be difficult and isolating. I found it essential to have someone who I trusted and could turn to when the going got tough – a mentor who understood my journey and could give me clarity and personalised advice.

You don't have to go it alone. I am here and available to help anytime you have questions about using the material contained within this workbook or if you have another matter you'd like assistance with.

To book a one-on-one *Personalised Guidance*
session with me, simply e-mail:
kylie@aguideforlife.com

Developing your tool kit

I also strongly advise you to start building a tool kit for your life journey. Following are some ideas.

Books

As you complete the curriculum in the *Workbook Series*, you will build a library of written resources: print and eBooks. I encourage you to read these books from start to finish, rather than just the prescribed sections needed to complete the workbook activities. Doing so will help you develop an appreciation of the journey you are on and provide you with a thorough understanding of how to successfully build a life you love. Most importantly these resources will help you comprehend just how powerful you truly are and assist you to unlock your unfulfilled potential, so you can fully express your magnificent, uninhibited self.

The following *Inspirational Resources* section provides a recommended reading list pertaining to the journey of self-discovery and uncovering your life purpose.

Audio

I find having something inspirational to listen to as I'm waking up with my first cup of tea sets my mood for the day. It also puts me to sleep of an evening and settles me down quickly if I'm having trouble going back to sleep in the middle of the night.

Consistently immersing yourself in self-help audio resources will help you transition from your current reality to a life in which you feel free to express every aspect of yourself. I suggest you choose audio books that align with the principles in this *Workbook Series*, as well as lectures and interviews with others who have successfully navigated the journey you are on.

You'll find plenty of recommendations to get you started in the *Inspirational Resources* section. Happy listening!

Power tools

Throughout the *Workbook Series* I recommend studying particular modalities and processes to help facilitate change in yourself and others. I like to think of these modalities and processes as 'power tools' for changing your reality. They are highly effective and simple to learn, and I promise you – they will come in handy if you find yourself having a meltdown in the middle of the night or your regular practitioner has a waiting list days-weeks-months long. Having these tools at your disposal will also save you a small fortune in the long run.

I'll also recommend practices that you can carry out at home to help you manage your emotions, particularly your fears. They will support you in overcoming your self-limiting mindset and self-destructive behaviours as you make the changes necessary to build a life that truly reflects you at your very core. *Check out the details of the series on the next page, and make sure you subscribe to my mailing list to know when the next workbook is released: kylie@aguideforlife. com. Subject line: 'Workbook Series'.*

I wish you well on your journey of self-discovery. Finding and living your purpose is the most gratifying and meaningful adventure you could ever take! Enjoy every moment and be as present as possible, regardless of the challenges you encounter. Trust your intuition. Take notice of the things that catch your attention, intrigue you, arouse your curiosity and evoke excitement.

My hope is that by sharing the resources and tools I have discovered, your hero's journey will be smoother and more direct. May your life be joyful, fulfilling and meaningful. Living your unique purpose will also elicit beneficial change in the lives of others and contribute to making the world a better place.

To living your purpose!
With love,

Kylie Xo

Kylie Attwell
www.aguideforlife.com

BUILD A LIFE YOU LOVE WORKBOOKS 1–7

Find Your Purpose, Change Your Life is the first in a series of seven *Build a Life You Love* workbooks designed to help you create a life in which you are free to express yourself fully across all aspects of your life. The topics covered in this series include:

Workbook #1

* the key to living a fulfilling, meaningful and joyous life

* the importance of developing an intimate relationship with yourself and how to do so

* the difference between purpose and passion

* the steps to take and the questions to ask yourself to uncover the themes of your life purpose.

Workbook #2

* why it's important to create an inspiring vision for your life that reflects your life purpose and expresses who you really are

* the role thoughts and emotions play in manifesting your dreams

- how to create a clear and exciting vision that feels tangible and real

- how to activate your vision and change your brain neurologically to match your desired new life.

Workbook #3

- why it's essential to clean up your life prior to taking any physical steps towards living your life purpose

- how to identify and eliminate aspects of your life that no longer serve you

- how to quickly and painlessly process the emotions that arise, particularly fear, guilt and deep sadness, as you start to leave the toxic people and aspects of your life behind.

Workbook #4

- the role your passions play in your daily life

- resources for uncovering and expressing your passions.

Workbook #5

- the mind-body connection, the relationship between the brain and the mind, and the role the conscious and subconscious minds play in making your dreams a reality

- why your day-to-day reality is simply a reflection of the story you have created about life, rather than what is true and indeed possible

- why certain types of unwanted experiences recur in your life, despite your efforts to change romantic partners, get a new job or move to a new location

- how the thinking-feeling-feeling-thinking cycle makes changing unwanted habits and self-destructive behaviour so difficult

- the power of the subconscious mind and the ways in which it can be quickly and effectively reprogrammed, so you can change your reality and experience the life you have always dreamed of

- recommended tools and techniques that will interrupt your habit of spiralling into negativity and depression

- an effective four-pronged approach for establishing a new mindset, letting go of your emotional baggage, creating a shift in your perception of life and adopting new functional patterns of behaviour.

Workbook #6

- exploration of the notion that Life is gently guiding, directing and communicating with you at all times, warning you not to take a particular direction or that the timing isn't quite right

- how to recognise and interpret the synchronicities, meaningful coincidences, messages and signs that Life is sending you.

Workbook #7

- why trying to control situations or the future, attempting to make something happen in your life or forcing an outcome actually pushes what you want further away

- effective techniques to help you surrender control, detach from the outcome and finally let go, so that the things you desire can begin to flow into your life.

If you would like to be advised when the next workbook in the series is released, please feel free to register your interest by e-mailing:

kylie@aguideforlife.com
Please use the subject heading 'Workbook Series'.
You will be contacted as soon as the latest workbook is published.

INSPIRATIONAL RESOURCES

Below are resources that I found invaluable for understanding WHY living your life purpose is the greatest gift you could give to both yourself and the planet. In addition, they will help you discover even more about yourself and provide you with examples of everyday people and historic icons who found and embodied their life purpose.

In saying that, I recommend you keep it simple for now and only explore these resources when instructed to do so or when you've finished working your way through the entire workbook.

RECOMMENDED READING

* *Emergence: Seven Steps for Radical Life Change* by Derek Rydall (Atria Books/Beyond Words 2015). Available in print and Kindle.

    In *Emergence*, Derek Rydall helps you recognise one simple, radical truth: the answer is already in you. Rydal believes that like an acorn has everything inside itself to become an oak tree, you have everything you need inside of yourself to fulfil your potential. In this seven-stage frame-work, Rydall shows you how to activate your genius within so you can fulfil your purpose in life.

- *Man's Search For Meaning* by Viktor E. Frankl (Ebury Publishing 2019). Available in print and Kindle.

  A prominent Viennese psychiatrist before the war, Viktor Frankl was uniquely able to observe the way that he and other inmates coped with the experience of being in Auschwitz. He noticed that it was the men who comforted others and who gave away their last piece of bread who survived the longest – and who offered proof that everything can be taken away from us except the ability to choose our attitude in any given set of circumstances. The sort of person the prisoner became was the result of an inner decision and not of camp influences alone. Only those who allowed their inner hold on their moral and spiritual selves to subside eventually fell victim to the camp's degenerating influence – whole those who made a victory of those experiences turned them into an inner triumph. Frankl came to believe that man's deepest desire is to search for meaning and purpose. This outstanding work offers us all a way to transcend suffering and find significance in the art of living.

- *Purpose: Find Your Why and the How Will Look After Itself* by Lisa Messenger (The Messenger Group 2018). Available in print and Kindle.

  In this soul-searching book Lisa discusses her own path to purpose, mixed with guidance and interviews from inspiring entrepreneurs and creatives who have followed their 'why' to a place of joy and fulfilment. Drawing on her own experiences and ground-breaking research that shows that a sense of purpose makes us happier, healthier and even live longer, Lisa encourages readers to find their illusive 'why'. With this they can reinvigorate their ambition, unleash their inner rebel and make a real impact in the world.

- *The Artist's Way: A Spiritual Path to Higher Creativity* by Julia Cameron (Souvenir Press 2012). Available in print and Kindle.

  The Artist's Way is an international bestseller that will take you on a twelve-week journey of self-discovery. It contains hundreds of highly effective exercises, many of which are designed to help you explore who you really are and what inspires you.

- *The Elephant Whisper: Learning About Life, Loyalty and Freedom from a Remarkable Herd of Elephants* by Lawrence Anthony (Pan Macmillan 2009). Available in print and Kindle.

  The Elephant Whisper is one of my favourite books. Not only does it demonstrate that 'purpose' comes in all shapes and sizes, but that there are threads of evidence woven throughout the fabric of our lives. This touching true story captures the lessons that can be learnt, the strength and resilience that can be demonstrated, the challenges that can be overcome, the magic and miracles that can occur, and the joy and fulfilment experienced when one embodies their life purpose.

- *The Miracle of a Definite Chief Aim* by Mitch Horowitz (G&D Media Corp 2019). Available in print and Kindle.

  What do you want most out of life? If you can answer that question with complete integrity and clarity, you are at the starting point of greatness. In his classic guides *Think and Grow Rich* and *The Laws of Success*, motivational pioneer Napoleon Hill taught that finding you Definite Chief Aim is the most decisive and important step you can take in life. In this compelling and eminently practical master class, acclaimed historian and New Thought author Mitch

Horowitz takes you for a deep dive inside Napoleon Hills most urgent principle. Through concrete techniques and examples, Mitch shows you how to identify your true aim, refine and act on it, and overcome setbacks.

- *The Path Made Clear: Discovering Your Life's Direction and Purpose* by Oprah Winfrey (Bluebird 2019). Available in print and Kindle.

Everyone has a purpose. And according to Oprah Winfrey, 'Your real job in life is to figure out as soon as possible what that is, who you are meant to be, and begin to honour your calling in the best way possible.' That journey starts right here.

In her latest book, *The Path Made Clear*, Oprah shares what she sees as a guide for activating your deepest vision of yourself, offering the framework for creating not just a life of success, but one of significance. The book's ten chapters are organised to help you recognise the important milestones along the road to self-discover, laying out what you really need in order to achieve personal contentment, and what life's detours are there to teach us.

Oprah opens each chapter by sharing her own key lessons and the personal stories that helped set the course for her best life. She then brings together wisdom and insights from luminaries in a wide array of fields, inspiring readers to consider what they're meant to do in the world and how to pursue it with passion and focus. These renowned figures share the greatest lessons from their own journeys towards a life filled with purpose.

Paired with over one hundred awe inspiring photographs to help illuminate the wisdom of these messages, *The Path*

Made Clear provide a beautiful resource for achieving a life lived in service of your calling – whatever it may be.

* *The Values Factor: The Secret to Creating an Inspired and Fulfilling Life* by Dr. John Demartini (Pub: Penguin Putnam Inc; I ed; 2013). Available in print and Kindle.

  Dr. Demartini's provocative thirteen-part questionnaire will reveal to you what you value most. Each chapter of this book then explains how to align every aspect of your life with your true values, so that you can finally achieve the success you were capable of all along.

RECOMMENDED LISTENING

Audible

Audible is a good resource for listening material. Because of the amount of audio material I devour, I find a monthly Audible subscription very cost effective. As a Gold Member, you receive your first audiobook for free and then receive one credit each month to download one audiobook of your choice. This membership also includes discounts on audiobooks, access to member-exclusive sales and Audible's Great Listen Guarantee, which allows you to swap the book you've purchased for another if you don't like it. It's slightly cheaper if you subscribe annually.

Below is a list of a few purpose related audio books to get you started:

* *Emergence: Seven Steps for Radical Life Change* by Derek Rydall, narrated by Derek Rydall (Tantor Audio 2015).

  In *Emergence*, Derek Rydall helps you recognise one simple, radical truth: the answer is already in you. Rydal believes that like an acorn has everything inside itself to become an oak tree, you have everything you need inside of yourself to fulfil your potential. In this seven-stage framework Rydall shows you how to activate the genius already in you so you can fulfil your purpose in life.

* *Man's Search For Meaning* by Viktor E. Frankl, narrated by Simon Vance (Blackstone Audio, Inc. 2004).

    A prominent Viennese psychiatrist before the war, Viktor Frankl was uniquely able to observe the way that he and other inmates coped with the experience of being in Auschwitz. He noticed that it was the men who comforted others and who gave away their last piece of bread who survived the longest – and who offered proof that everything can be taken away from us except the ability to choose our attitude in any given set of circumstances. The sort of person the prisoner became was the result of an inner decision and not of camp influences alone. Only those who allowed their inner hold on their moral and spiritual selves to subside eventually fell victim to the camp's degenerating influence – whole those who made a victory of those experiences turned them into an inner triumph. Frankl came to believe that man's deepest desire is to search for meaning and purpose. This outstanding work offers us all a way to transcend suffering and find significance in the art of living.

* *The Miracle of a Definite Chief Aim* by Mitch Horowitz, narrated by Mitch Horowitz (Gildan Media, LLC 2017).

    What do you want most out of life? If you can answer that question with complete integrity and clarity, you are at the starting point of greatness. In his classic guides *Think and Grow Rich* and *The Laws of Success*, motivational pioneer Napoleon Hill taught that finding you Definite Chief Aim is the most decisive and important step you can take in life. In this compelling and eminently practical master class, acclaimed historian and New Thought author Mitch Horowitz takes you for a deep dive inside Napoleon Hills most urgent principle. Through concrete techniques and examples, Mitch shows you how to identify your true aim, refine and act on it, and overcome setbacks.

* *The Path Made Clear: Discovering Your Life's Direction and Purpose* by Oprah Winfrey, narrated by Oprah Winfrey and full cast (Macmillan Digital Audio 2019). Available in print, audio and Kindle.

Everyone has a purpose. And according to Oprah Winfrey, 'Your real job in life is to figure out as soon as possible what that is, who you are meant to be, and begin to honour your calling in the best way possible.' That journey starts right here.

In her latest book, *The Path Made Clear*, Oprah shares what she sees as a guide for activating your deepest vision of yourself, offering the framework for creating not just a life of success, but one of significance. The book's ten chapters are organised to help you recognise the important milestones along the road to self-discover, laying out what you really need in order to achieve personal contentment, and what life's detours are there to teach us.

Oprah opens each chapter by sharing her own key lessons and the personal stories that helped set the course for her best life. She then brings together wisdom and insights from luminaries in a wide array of fields, inspiring readers to consider what they're meant to do in the world and how to pursue it with passion and focus. These renowned figures share the greatest lessons from their own journeys towards a life filled with purpose.

Read by Oprah Winfrey and a full cast including Adyashanti, Alanis Morrissette, Amy Purdy, Barbara Brown Taylor, Bishop T. D. Jakes, Brene Brown, Brian Grazer, Brother David Steindl-rast, Bryan Stevenson, Carole Bayer Sager, Caroline Myss, Charles Eisenstein, Cheryl Strayed, Cicely Tyson, Cindy Crawford, Dani Shapiro, Daniel Pink, David Brooks, Debbie Ford, Deepak Chopra, Dr. Shefali Tsabary, Eckhart Tolle, Elizabeth Gilbert, Elizabeth Lesser, Ellen Degeneres, Fr. Richard Rohr, Gabrielle Bernstein, Gary Zukav, Glennon Doyle, Goldie Hawn, India.Arie, Iyanla Vanzant, Jack Canfield, Jane Fonda, Janet Mock, Jay-Z, Jean Houston, Jeff Weiner, Vice President Joe Biden, Joel Osteen, U.S. Congressman John Lewis, Jon Bon Jovi, Jon Kabat-Zinn, Jordan Peele, Kerry Washington, Lin-Manuel Miranda, Lynne Twist, Marianne Williamson, Mark Nepo, Michael Bernard Beckwith, Michael Singer, Mindy Kaling, Mitch Albom, Nate Berkus, Pastor A. R. Bernard, Pema Chodron, President Jimmy Carter, Rev. Ed Bacon, Rob Bell, Robin Roberts, RuPaul Charles, Sarah Ban Breathnach, Shauna Niequist, Shawn Achor, Shonda Rhimes, Sidney Poitier, Sister Joan Chittister, Stephen Colbert, Sue Monk Kidd, T. D. Jakes, Thich Nhat Hanh, Thomas Moore, Tim Storey, Tracey Jackson, Tracy McMillan, Tracy Morgan, Trevor Noah, Wes Moore, William Paul Young and Wintley Phipps.

- *The Values Factor: The Secret to Creating an Inspired and Fulfilling Life* by Dr. John Demartini, narrated by Erik Synnestyedt (Gildan Media, LLC 2013).

    Dr. Demartini's provocative thirteen-part questionnaire will reveal to you what you value most. Each chapter of this book then explains how to align every aspect of your life with your true values, so that you can finally achieve the success you were capable of all along.

YouTube

I also search YouTube for lectures by my favourite teachers for other sources of a morning and bedtime inspiration. These of course are free.

You Can Heal Your Life Summit by Hay House

I recommend you subscribe to the Hay House annual *Your Can Heal Your Life Summit* (formally known as the *Hay House World Summit*). It starts in May every year, runs for ten days and is free to join. You will have access to intimate conversations with 100 of the world's leading personal transformation experts, where they share lessons learned and the wisdom gained from living their life purpose. There are also movies to watch, powerful guided meditations and exercises to help you create shifts from the inside out, along with tips and techniques to inspire confidence and clarity. When you join, you receive instant access to bonus audio lessons and will be the first to know about special offerings. You can get a taste of what this summit has to offer by listening to the mini weekly lessons offered by the *Hay House World Summit Podcast*. Check it out at: www.youcan-healyourlifesummit.com

Podcasts

A podcast is a method of broadcasting audio (and video) files. You can download and listen to Podcasts on any 'smart device'. But first you'll need to download a podcast app such as:

- Podcasts (free, only available for Apple products)

- Pocket Casts (one off fee to purchase the app)

- Spotify (monthly subscription fee).

When you find a favourite podcast, you can receive new podcasts automatically by 'subscribing'. In the meantime, here are a few recommendations to get you started.

- *Aubrey Marcus Podcast*

  Founder of Onnit and modern philosopher Aubrey Marcus asks the important questions: How do we find our purpose, wake up to who we truly are, have a few more laughs, and human being a little better? The Aubrey Marcus Podcasts bring in world class quests from the fields of athletics, health, business, fitness, science, relationship and spirituality, and asks them to open up to the failures and success that define their wisdom and character.

  (*Warning: this podcast occasionally contains coarse language and swearing.*)

- *Good Life Project*

  Inspirational, intimate and disarmingly unfiltered conversations about living a fully engaged, fiercely connected and meaning-drenched life. From iconic world-shakers like Elizabeth Gilbert, Sir Ken Robinson, Seth Godin and Gretchen Rubin to everyday guests, every story matters.

- *Hay House World Summit*

  Offers you weekly mini lessons as a taste of what you can hear during the annual You Can Heal Your Life Summit.

- *Hay House Live!*

  Enjoy insightful and inspiring lectures from *Hay House Live!* events featuring leading experts in the fields of alternative health, nutrition, intuitive medicine, psychology, spirituality, success and personal development. This podcast program will help you get motivated to live your best life possible and open your mind to some new ideas.

* *Life on Purpose*

How do you live your life more deliberately? What can you do to bring more meaning and purpose into your life? How does that affect your health, happiness and well-being? If you are asking those questions, you're in the right place. *Life on Purpose* host Gregory Berg presents in-depth conversations with entrepreneurs, creatives, seekers and thought leaders from around the world.

* *Oprah's SuperSoul Conversations*

Awaken to discover and connect the deeper meaning of the world around you with *SuperSoul*. Hear Oprah's personal selection of her interviews with thought-leaders, best-selling authors, spiritual luminaries, as well as health and wellness experts. All designed to light you up, guide you through life's big questions and help bring you closer to your best self.

* *TED Radio Hour*

The *TED Radio Hour* is a journey through fascinating ideas: astonishing inventions, fresh approaches to old problems, new ways to think and create. Based on Talks given by riveting speakers on the world-renowned TED stage, each show is centred on a common theme such as the source of happiness, crowed-sourcing innovation, power shifts or inexplicable connections. The *TED Radio Hour* is hosted by Guy Raz and is a co-production of NPR and TED.

* *The Daily Boost*

The Daily Boost is for people who aspire to live a better life and find themselves confused, frustrated and not knowing what steps to take. Host, Scott Smith, will help give you the motivation you need to clarify your purpose, eliminate confusion, create your plan and become unstoppable!

- *The Dr. John Demartini Show*

    Dr. Demartini discusses the importance of getting in touch with one's higher purpose and finding work that is congruent with your value system.

- *The Tony Robbins Podcast*

    'Why live an ordinary life when you can live an extraordinary one?' In this podcast, Tony Robbins shares proven strategies and tactics so you can achieve massive results in your business, relationships, health and finances. In addition to excerpts from his signature events and other exclusive, never-before-released audio content, Tony and his team also conduct deeply insightful interviews with the most prominent masterminds and experts on the global stage.

- *The Unmistakable Creative*

    Hailed as a cross between TEDTalks and Oprah. Eliminate the feeling of being stuck in your life, blocked in your creativity, and discover higher levels of meaning and purpose in your life and career. Listen to deeply personal, insightful and thought-provoking stories from the world's leading thinkers and doers including best-selling authors, artists, peak performance psychologists, happiness researchers, artists, venture capitalists and even former bank robbers.

- *True Calling Project*

    John Harrison is a professional psychotherapist and coach. He brings his insight and experience from his former career as a military officer, 9–5 office worker, and his current careers as a therapist and coach in interviews with professionals, psychology experts and those living their higher potential. Each week you'll get discussion stories and insights on finding your 'why', how to optimise your life and business, and the mental and emotional challenges that can keep you stuck. He and his guests explore the practical and spiritual aspects of engaging in a satisfying career and a meaningful life.

RECOMMENDED VIEWING

TED Talks

* *The Power of Purpose* by Steve Taylor

www.youtube.com/watch?v=LIyLzeDpHm0

In this TED Talk, senior lecturer in psychology at Leeds Beckett University and best- selling author, Steve Taylor, explores the power that purpose has in our life.

He believes the reason purpose is crucial is because it creates motivation, orientation, resilience and positivity in our lives. Without purpose, he says, it's easy for us to feel adrift and disorientated and we become more vulnerable to boredom, anxiety and depression.

It is his view that a strong sense of purpose has a powerful positive effect. We feel part of something bigger than ourselves, more energetic and optimistic, and there's a background reason for everything we do, he says. He believes a sense of purpose is essential for our psychological health, regardless of whether it's personal accumulative, altruistic or idealistic, self-developmental or transpersonal.

However, he believes that it's only when we possess a deep authentic sense of purpose that our lives really become the most fulfilling, most productive and most meaningful. It's not about going out and finding a purpose, but through uncovering our purpose, which he says is already inside us but we may not have already gained access to due social pressures, lack of courage or because we haven't been living authentically.

* *How to Unlock the Power of Purpose* by Richard Leider (TEDxEdina)

www.youtube.com/watch?v=sfiToT6S0j8

According to Richard Leider, who is ranked by Forbes as one of the 'Top 5' most respected executive coaches and founder of Inventure – The Purpose Company, our reason for getting up in the morning is not only essential, it's fundamental to our health and happiness.

'Imagine a pill', he says, 'that would aid cognitive decline by 40–50%, reduce macroscopic stroke by 40%, aid sleep and sleep apnoea, and add seven years to your life. How much do you think this pill would cost?'

'That pill,' he says, 'is free and available to all. It's called purpose.'

Richard believes that your calling is when you bring your gifts, your passions and your values together into your work and your life. You'll be fundamentally happier, he says, if you bring your calling to what you do.

Are you using your gifts on the things you feel passionate about in an environment that fits your values? That's the bottom line today of happiness, fulfilment, productivity and many other things.

- *How to Find Work You Love* by Scott Dinsmore

  www.youtube.com/watch?v=jpe-LKn-4gM

  Scott Dinsmore is a career change strategist whose mission is to change the world by helping people find what excites them and build a career around the work only they are capable of doing. In this TED Talk, he discusses how he made the transition from a miserable carer as an employee in a Fortune 500 company to living his life purpose as the Founder of Live Your Legend, a career and connection platform to inspire people to find their passion. During his presentation he shares his Passionate Work Framework – three surprisingly simple practices for finding and doing work you love, that all happen to be completely within our control. He makes his career tools available free to the public through his community at:

  www.liveyourlegend.net

- *To Find Work You Love, Don't Follow Your Passion* by Benjamin Todd

  www.youtube.com/watch?v=MKlxlDLa9EA

  Benjamin Todd, the co-founder and Executive Director of 80,000 Hours, an Oxford-based charity dedicated to helping people find fulfilling careers that make a real difference, doesn't believe that we should take the mainstream media advice that tells us to 'follow our passion'.

  In this TEDx talk, he explains the research behind why this advice is dead wrong. Based on the research 80,000 Hours had done with academics at Oxford, he believes that instead of asking what our own interests and passions are, we should be focusing much more on what we can do for other people and to make the world a better place. His single slogan career advice is: Do what's valuable.

He says that, even if you were to match your passion with your work and were successful, you'll fail to have a fulfilling career if the work you do isn't meaningful. He believes that you shouldn't just follow your passion to find the work you love. The secret to a fulfilling career, he says, is to focus on getting good at something that genuinely helps others and makes the world a better place.

He shares two of the key ingredients that have been identified for doing what is valuable, along with three practical steps you can take to help you do something valuable in your career. He says that by implementing these principles, fulfilment and a passionate career will emerge.

- *Finding Clarity in Your Calling* by Robbie Osenga (TEDxNormal)

www.youtube.com/watch?v=7WJ-jMmyIbw

Career coach and motivational speaker, Robbie Osenga, believes that in order to find our true calling we need to examine each of the puzzle pieces of our lives. In this TEDx Talk, he breaks down his Clarity in Calling process, which involves identifying the highs and lows that have shaped your life; recognising your true strengths and your true weaknesses, what is most meaningful to you, what you want to be true in your life ten years and then one year from now; and determining what you need to do in order to make what you want to be true in your life happen.

He says that once you have worked through this process, the most important and essential thing you need to do is to give yourself permission to live your calling.

- *2005 Stanford Commencement Address* by Steve Jobs

  www.youtube.com/watch?v=UF8uR6Z6KLc

  Drawing from some of the most pivotal points in his life, Steve Jobs (Dec. 5.10.2011), chief executive officer and co-founder of Apple Computer and of Pixar Animation Studios, urges 2005 Stanford graduates to pursue their dreams and see the opportunities in life's setbacks – including death itself – at the University's 114th Commencement on June 12, 2005.

Documentaries

- *Discover the Gift (2012)*

  Within each of us, there are special gifts simply awaiting discovery. The sense of joy, power, fulfilment, freedom and unconditional love that we experience in our lives is directly related to these gifts, yet so many of us have yet to unlock their full potential, leaving us longing for a sense of happiness and fulfilment.

  For sister and brother team Shajen Joy Aziz and Demian Licthenstein, something was missing in their lives until they tapped into the power of their own unique gifts, leading to a profound personal transformation that has enabled them to connect to the fullness of life. Their incredible personal journeys of spiritual growth have fuelled their desire to share what they have learned. In this feature-length inspirational documentary, they take us step by step through their journey of discovery, which has the power to change not only individual lives but to transform the world.

- *Finding Joe (2011)*

  A film about famed mythologist, Joseph Campbell's, hero's journey and following your bliss.

- *May I Be Frank (2010)*

  Ex-Addict Frank Ferrante is a 54-year-old, overweight Sicilian-American from Brooklyn with Hepatitis C, some bad health habits and an unquenchable appetite for women. He also wants to fall in love one more time before he dies. *May I Be Frank*, documents Fran's transformation as he stumbles into the aptly named vegan Café Gratitude and over 42 days begins a life-changing journey. During this he is coached physically, emotionally and spiritually by three twenty-something staff members on the path to enlightenment. Challenged by years of addiction, fatigue and family dysfunction, Frank's quest for a healthier lifestyle is both tense and touching. Through his metamorphosis, we witness the powerful effects of change upon one person's life and the potential we all have to find the most important love of all – love of ourselves.

- *Project Happiness (2011)*

  This documentary follows students from three continents – North America, Africa and Asia – as they search for the meaning of 'lasting happiness'. Included in the film is footage of interviews conducted by the students with renowned scientists, celebrities and world political and spiritual leaders.

Biographies

- *Erin Brockovich (2000)*

  Erin Brockovich (Julia Roberts) is a woman in a tight spot. Following a car accident in which Erin is not a fault, Erin pleads with her attorney Ed Masry (Albert Finney) to hire her at his law firm. Erin stumbles upon some medical records placed in real estate files. She convinces Ed to allow her to investigate, where she discovers a cover-up involving contaminated water in a local community that is causing devastating illnesses among its residents.

- *First Man (2018)*

  The riveting story of NASA's mission to land a man on the moon, focusing on Neil Armstrong and the years 1961–1969. A visceral, first-personal account, based on the book by James R. Hansen, the movie explores the sacrifices and the cost – on Armstrong and on the nation – of one of the most dangerous missions in history.

- *Hidden Figures (2016)*

  Three brilliant African-American women at NASA – Katherine Johnson (Taraji P. Henson), Dorothy Vaughan (Octavia Spencer) and Mary Jackson (Janelle Monáe) – serve as the brains behind one of the greatest operations in history: the launch of astronaut John Glenn (Glen Powell) into orbit, a stunning achievement that restored the nation's confidence, turned around the Space Race and galvanised the world.

- *Jobs (2013)*

  College dropout Steve Jobs (Ashton Kutcher), together with his friend, technical whiz-kid Steve Wozniak (Josh Gad), sparks a revolution in home computers with the invention of the Apple I in 1976. Built in the garage of Jobs' parents, the device – and the subsequent formation of Apple Inc. – have changed the world for all time. Though he is viewed as a visionary, Jobs' tenure as Apple's leader is a rocky one, leading to his eventual ouster from the company he co-founded.

- *Mandela: Long Walk to Freedom (2013)*

   The remarkable life of South African revolutionary, president and world icon Nelson Mandela (Idris Elba) takes centre stage. Though he had humble beginnings as a herd boy in rural village, Mandela became involved in the anti-apartheid movement and co-founded the African National Congress Youth League. His activities eventually led to his imprisonment on Robben Island from 1964 to 1990. In 1994, Mandela became the first president of democratic South Africa

- *Milk (2008)*

   In 1972, Harvey Milk (Sean Penn) and his then-lover Scott Smith leave New York for San Francisco, with Milk determined to accomplish something meaningful in his life. Settling in the Castro District, he opens a camera shop and helps transform the area into a mecca for gays and lesbians. In 1977, he becomes the nation's first openly gay man elected to a notable public office when he wins a seat on the Board of Supervisors. The following year, Dan White (Josh Brolin) kills Milk in cold blood.

- *Selma (2014)*

   Although the Civil Rights Act of 1964 legally desegregated the South, discrimination was still rampant in certain areas, making it very difficult for black Americans to register to vote. In 1965, an Alabama city become the battleground in the fight for suffrage. Despite violent opposition, Dr Martin Luther King Jr. (David Oyelowo) and his followers pressed forward on an epic march from Selma to Montgomery, and their efforts culminated in President Lyndon Johnson signing the Voting Rights Act of 1965.

- *The Motorcycle Diaries (2004)*

    On a break before his last semester of medical school, Ernesto 'Che' Guevara (Gael Garcia Bernal) travels with this friend Alberto Granado (Rodrigo De la Serna) from Brazil to Peru by motorcycle. The two men soon witness the great disparities in South America, encountering poor peasants and observing the exploitation of labour by wealthy industrialists. When they reach a leper colony in Peru, Ernesto's values have changed so much that he sides with the sufferers, forgetting his own comfort.

Drama

- *Hector and the Search for Happiness (2014)*

    Disillusioned with the tedium of his existence, psychiatrist Hector (Simon Pegg) confesses to his girlfriend (Rosamund Pike) that he feels he is a fraud for dispensing recommendation to patients who never seem to improve or get any happier. He considers breaking out of his lacklustre routine. Summoning up some courage, Hector gives his staved curiosity free rein and embarks on an international quest to find the right formula to bring him joy and vitality.

- *The Shift (2009)*

    In this compelling film, Dr Wayne W. Dyer explores the spiritual journey from ambition to meaning. The powerful shift from the ego constructs we are taught early in life by parents and society – which promotes and emphasises achievement and accumulation – are shown in contrast to a life of meaning, focused on serving and giving back. Through the intertwined stories of an overachieving businessman, a mother of two seeking her own expression in the world and a director trying to make a name for him, this entertaining film not only inspires but also teaches us how to create a life of meaning and purpose.

- *The Help (2011)*

    In 1960s Mississippi, Southern society girl Skeeter (Emma Stone) returns from college with dreams of being a writer. She turns her small town on its ear by choosing to interview the black women who have spent their lives taking care of prominent white families. Only Aibileen (Viola Davis), the housekeeper of Skeeter's best friend, will talk first. But as the pair continue the collaboration, more women decide to come forward, and as it turns out, they have quite a lot to say.

NOTE FROM THE AUTHOR

I trust you enjoyed the discovery process. I'm looking forward to hearing your aha moments!

Feel free to e-mail me or post them on Facebook so the *A Guide for Life* community can be inspired and benefit from your insights.

kylie@aguideforlife.com
www.facebook.com/aguideforlife